"I'm in a sprint season right now. Lo of things going wrong, lots of thing going right. I grabbed Sarah's book, sa down, and took a deep breath. Then I exhaled. Her words felt like a cool glass of water on a scorching hot day, like an invitation to come away and rest for a while. You can't read through these pages and feel stressed at the same time. She writes beautifully, lyrically, and biblically. If you've been running too fast for too long, or if you want to avoid the rat race altogether, give yourself some time to rest, be refreshed, and soak in the wisdom God has imparted to Sarah. This is a beautiful book."

Susie Larson, show host, author, national speaker

"Living in our fast-paced society, we, as Christian women, need to slow down and experience the spiritual rest, refreshment, and retreat Sarah talks about in *Whispers and Wildflowers*. We need to withdraw from the busyness of life to spend undistracted time with the One who created us. Thank you, Sarah, for writing this thirty-day devotional and pointing us back toward Jesus. The two of us love it and plan to pass it along to the GirlDefined sisterhood!"

Kristen Clark and Bethany Beal, cofounders of GirlDefined Ministries; authors of *Girl Defined* and *Love Defined*

"A thirty-day retreat sounds impossible for the modern woman. Sarah Beth Marr knows this, yet she has created a tool to usher today's woman into daily retreat by making space to absorb

reflect on how God is at work. This is a book about noticing both the quiet whispers and the flowers found in desolate places . . . the wildflowers."

Alexandra Kuykendall, author of *Loving My Actual Life*; cohost of *The Open Door Sisterhood* podcast

"*Whispers and Wildflowers* is a retreat for the soul. It offers those in need of fresh rest, hope, and recovery a chance to lay down and see the goodness of God."

Kelly Balarie, author of *Battle Ready* and *Fear Fighting*; blogger at *Purposeful Faith*; national speaker; host of The Journey Together Summit

"As a gardener, I wholly appreciate Sarah Beth Marr's dive into horticultural metaphors to lead us all closer to the Gardener of our souls. This thirty-day journey, powered by Sarah's keen insight and a heart that is so obviously close to Jesus, will woo you to Him in new ways."

Mary DeMuth, author of *Jesus Every Day*

"If you find yourself in a place of hurried pace with a crowded soul, then Sarah Beth Marr's daily devotionals in *Whispers and Wildflowers* will offer the space and healing you need. With a calm, inviting voice, she echoes God's whispers and centers your heart on the truth of who Christ is and what He does to grow the good things in your life."

Heather MacFadyen, host of the *God Centered Mom* podcast; creator of Don't Mom Alone Community

"With blissful insights, Sarah Beth Marr reminds us that God's mercies are new every morning. Great is His faithfulness. In each devotional chapter, Sarah honestly shares her journey toward a deeper relationship with God. But most of all, she encourages us to relax and rest in the arms of a loving and attentive Creator. He whispers to us. He refreshes us in His well-watered spiritual garden. Sarah assures us we can trust in God's Word and lavish care as we return to our busy lives, renewed and secured from within."

Judith Couchman, speaker, professor, and author of *Designing a Woman's Life*

"*Whispers and Wildflowers* is a gracious invitation to come away and enjoy the sweetest gifts of our Savior. Sarah Beth Marr digs deep, breathing fresh insight into rich metaphors of faith and communion. She writes, '[Jesus] knows the best refreshment for our weary souls is Himself.' And Sarah knows how to gently lead us to Him. I look forward to many more quiet moments of listening for His whispers with this inspiring devotional."

Kim Hyland, author of *An Imperfect Woman*

"As our lives seem to move at a frenetic pace, we rarely take the time to spiritually recover. Our hearts and minds yearn for the refreshment and rest of spending intimate time with the Father and savoring His unfailing love for us. Sarah Beth Marr invites us to that restful place through a beautiful thirty-day

journey of renewal. *Whispers and Wildflowers* is like a cup of cool water for a thirsty soul."

Karol Ladd, bestselling author of *The Power of a Positive Woman*

"We need *Whispers and Wildflowers*. We need the rest it offers, we need the slow it calls us to, and we desperately need the calm closeness to God it beckons us toward. Sarah is a gentle truth teller and a much-needed guide in the middle of our busy and cluttered world. This book gives us the soothing prompt that our souls so desperately yearn for: Daughter, come and rest."

Maria Furlough, author of *Breaking the Fear Cycle*

"This book is for any woman who needs a hard reset for her soul. Sarah's honesty, words, and lessons penned in these pages are a blessing to the weary heart."

Jordan Lee Dooley, author of *Purpose*

"With tenderness and intentionality, Sarah Beth Marr offers a retreat for our souls in *Whispers and Wildflowers*. Sometimes we feel we need permission to exhale the craziness of life, draw near to Jesus, and simply be still. Let this book be that for your heart today."

Stacey Thacker, speaker and author of *When Grace Walks In*

"If you are looking for a retreat for your soul, this is the book for you!"

Katie Norris, founder of Fotolanthropy & Fotostrap; producer of two award-winning documentaries, *Travis: A Soldier's Story* and *The Luckiest Man*

WHISPERS and WILDFLOWERS

30 Days to Slow Your Pace,
Savor Scripture
& Draw Closer to God

Sarah Beth Marr

BakerBooks

a division of Baker Publishing Group
Grand Rapids, Michigan

© 2019 by Pointe to Grace

Published by Baker Books
a division of Baker Publishing Group
PO Box 6287, Grand Rapids, MI 49516-6287
www.bakerbooks.com

Printed in the United States of America

Library of Congress Cataloging-in-Publication Data
Names: Marr, Sarah Beth, 1979– author.
Title: Whispers and wildflowers : 30 days to slow your pace, savor scripture & draw closer to God / Sarah Beth Marr.
Description: Grand Rapids, MI : Baker Books, [2019]
Identifiers: LCCN 2018026528 | ISBN 9780801073090 (pbk.)
Subjects: LCSH: Christian women—Religious life. | Christian women—Prayers and devotions.
Classification: LCC BV4527 .M2644 2019 | DDC 248.8/43—dc23
LC record available at https://lccn.loc.gov/2018026528

The author is represented by The Steve Laube Agency, Phoenix, AZ. (www.stevelaube.com)

To the readers

May God stir up your joy, deepen your peace,
and meet you here in these pages. Each
of you is an answer to my prayers.

CONTENTS

Contents

INTRODUCTION

My heart is steady, God; my heart is steady.
I will sing and praise you.
Wake up, my soul.

PSALM 57:7–8 NCV

I LONG TO LIVE MY WHOLE LIFE with focus, a clear mission, and a steady heart. I long to dance with genuine freedom the dance God gave me—fully in the moment and enjoying every step. I long to be right in tune with God, listening carefully to His voice and keeping in step with His directing hand. I long to be who I truly am, to deeply enjoy what I am doing, and to impact my sphere of influence with the love of Christ. I long for that singular focus to ebb out into my living and be reflected in my actions. I long to passionately enjoy the Word daily. I long to grow so close to Jesus that my heart experiences the full depth of His peace and joy. I long to feel the deep satisfaction of a life connected to Jesus: focused on my mission, steady in my heart, and joy overflowing.

But a lot of days I feel distracted, overwhelmed, busy, cluttered, and tired. The information, emails, social media, and busy calendars overload me. All the clutter drowns out God's voice, depleting my joy, stirring up discontentment, robbing me of abundant life, and making me feel discouraged, numb, or inwardly chaotic. I grow desensitized to the fact that when I fill the pauses in my day with more clutter, I miss God and miss experiencing the well of joy He has planted inside me. On those days, I feel like I am missing the focus that I was designed for but cannot seem to find. Maybe you feel it too. If you do, I know you desire to dance through your life in step with God. I know you are weary from the pull of distractions, to-do lists, pressures, expectations, full calendars, and constant activity. You may feel depleted and crave a more satisfying and joy-filled life.

This earth-life has always been noisy, demanding, and hectic. It goes back to Eve in the garden. She was distracted by the enticements of the world and the enemy's taunts; they interrupted her oneness with the Father. In our lives, God knows it is a challenge to maintain that garden intimacy with the Lord because not only are we bombarded with distractions and busyness, but the enemy of our souls is also doing everything he can to steal abundant life from us.

I wrote this book as a thirty-day retreat to enjoy day by day. My hope is that it helps you slow your pace, savor Scripture, and ultimately draw closer to God. But gals, if you do what I do sometimes and get lost in a book and read it in two days, that is great too! If journaling helps you soak in truth and the lessons you want to remember, keep a journal close and scribble down the things that tug at your heart the most. These daily retreats with Jesus will involve a bit of weed pulling, some tending and digging, and lots of soul-nourishment and growth as we linger with the Lord. As the

Master Gardener, He wants your life to blossom in all its beauty and flourish from a deeply planted root system of a precious relationship with Him. He wants to meet with you, encourage you, nurture you, and guide you so that the garden of your life in Him is healthy and flourishing. Consider these retreats with Him to be little meetings in which you bring your heart out from the fog of busyness, distractions, and clutter and back into the arms of the tender of your soul.

> You did it: you changed wild lament
>   into whirling dance;
> You ripped off my black mourning band
>   and decked me with wildflowers.
> I'm about to burst with song;
>   I can't keep quiet about you.
> GOD, my God,
>   I can't thank you enough. (Ps. 30:11–12, Message)

This book is an invitation to pull in close to God so we can experience the whirling kind of dancing . . . wildflowers and all. I love that God inspired David, the author of this psalm, to use the word *dance* in this verse. David didn't write that God turned his mourning into walking/running/climbing a hill . . . (you get the idea). No, he wrote that God turned his mourning into dancing.

There is something about dancing. It invites a freedom, an act of letting go, a celebration. If you read my first book, *Dreaming with God: A Bold Call to Step Out and Follow God's Lead*, you know my background is in professional ballet. Dancing finds its way into my writing because it's what I spent most of my life doing, from the time I was nine years old until just a couple of years ago. I have a heart for dancing, but I've realized that so many women can relate to it whether or not they studied ballet as a little girl. I have discovered that dancing is a beautiful metaphor for our walk with God. In a sense, when we let Him lead our dance, our lives flow in beautiful synchronicity with Him, and we experience abundant life and the dreams He created just for us. My prayer is that whether or not you are a dancer, your heart will be brought back to a place of "whirling dance" as you slow your pace, savor Scripture, and draw closer to God. God wants to remove all that weighs down your heart, mind, and soul and to lavish you with abundant life.

Until recently, I had only seen Psalm 30:11–12 translated this way: "You turned my lament into dancing; You removed my sackcloth and clothed me with gladness, so that I can sing to You and not be silent. Lord my God, I will praise You forever" (HCSB). So when I ran across *The Message* version, with the wildflowers and whirling dance, it sparked something in my heart God wanted me to pay attention to. His gladness and joy for us could easily be missed if we do not carefully guard and tend our hearts and give our hearts to Him. When we make a habit of drawing close to our Savior throughout both the busy and the quiet moments of our day, our hearts grow fully alive. Whirling dance. And we experience the full measure of God's love, joy, and grace. Decked with wildflowers. And I'm learning that when we fully tune in to God, we can hear His whispers better. When we grow quiet, His whispers become more clear. And when we hear His whispers, we live differently—fully alive and flourishing. We gain so much when we draw close to God.

- We hear from Him.
- We gain a rootedness.
- We are filled so we can pour out.
- We find the greatest rest.
- We discover our gifts.
- We discover His will.
- We become fully alive.

These are just some of the things we are going to discover as we navigate these pages together.

When Jesus walked the earth, He showed us how to live. His world was busy, crowded with folks who wanted to experience His healing touch and divine words. His life was real—He had work to do, obligations and chores to tend to, not to mention a great purpose to fulfill. He had the distractions of the naysayers around Him, all sorts of people watching Him with eyebrows raised, and the enemy of all our souls doing everything he could to tempt Jesus to give up on His mission. So while His busyness was different from our modern-day forms of busyness, He did have the weight of the whole world on His shoulders. What did Jesus do when He felt all the noise closing in on Him? Instead of pushing through it and keeping on keeping on, He withdrew . . . He retreated. He put everything on hold and ran to His Father's embrace. He set the world aside and placed Himself in the presence of the One who was in control. He knew He would soon need to return to His life, but He also knew when His heart needed to retreat to the Father's love and tending.

Jesus's heart stayed healthy because of those retreats with God. He found the strength, fuel, and perspective He needed for His earth-life there in those quiet moments with God. He returned refreshed and filled up. His load didn't change, but His ability to handle it well did. His mission was great, but He could not accomplish it without this regular retreating. His retreats with the Father kept Him on His mission and ultimately helped Him fulfill it.

Dictionary.com defines *retreat* as "(1) the forced or strategic withdrawal of an army or an armed force before an enemy; (2) the act of withdrawing, as into safety or privacy; retirement; seclusion; (3) a place of refuge, seclusion, or privacy" and "to withdraw, retire, or draw back."[1]

Jesus exemplified how we are to find true life, and one of the ways He did that is by modeling this retreating. Today begins a strategic withdrawal from the demands, stress, and distractions that are depleting our hearts and souls.

We are women of a fast-paced generation, and it can feel counterintuitive to draw back, to apply the brakes on our lives, to pull over and retreat with Jesus. It can feel like if we pause, our lives will get behind, we will miss something, or we will be left in the dust. But dancing with God at His pace will look and feel different from the rest of the world. In a way that only God can accomplish, He will refresh you when you retreat with Him. Often we create the habit of pressing through our feelings of busyness and overwhelmedness, which only leaves us more depleted. Sometimes we are so cluttered in our souls that we do not realize how much we crave to be with God. Sometimes we run to the very things that are depleting our souls instead of running to God. Sometimes we miss out on the bread of the Word that gives life to our hearts. If we do not retreat daily with Jesus, we will miss out on bread and water for our hungry and thirsty souls.

Today I invite you to strategically withdraw the best you can to focus on the One who has your life in His hands. I invite you to curl up close to the One who wants to refresh, refuel, and realign your heart. Each daily reading is a guide to help you retreat with Jesus so you can experience His peace, joy, and renewal in a fresh way and grow in the habit of abiding in Christ throughout your whole day. God has a mission and purpose for your life, your current season, and even your day. May the verses below inspire your heart for the journey ahead:

> The eternal God is your refuge, and underneath are the everlasting arms. (Deut. 33:27 NIV)

> Keep company with GOD, get in on the best. (Ps. 37:4 Message)

> God is our refuge and strength, a helper who is always found in times of trouble. (Ps. 46:1 HCSB)

> Pile your troubles on GOD's shoulders—he'll carry your load, he'll help you out. (Ps. 55:22 Message)

> I will say of the LORD, "He is my refuge and my fortress, my God, in whom I trust." (Ps. 91:2 NIV)

> Find a quiet, secluded place . . . Just be there as simply and honestly as you can manage. The focus will shift from you to God, and you will begin to sense his grace. (Matt. 6:6 Message)

> We who have fled for refuge might have strong encouragement to seize the hope set before us. (Heb. 6:18 HCSB)

This book is an anthem for my own heart and, I hope, a gentle invitation to yours. Just so we're clear, I'm not going to force you to go back to using a flip phone, deactivate your social media account, erase every activity from your calendar, or live in a bubble. I definitely don't want to give busyness a bad rap either. We were meant for good works (see Eph. 2:10). We were designed to move, live, work, and create. There is nothing bad about work, our phones, social media, or a busy calendar. But sometimes we get so caught up in all that stuff that we tend to miss out on the peace, joy, and intimacy God has for us. And I don't want us to miss it. I don't want us to miss Him anymore. Instead, I want us to experience and own a new joy as we tend to our souls, tune in to God, and truly flourish in Him. Retreating is one thing, but God knows we have to go back to our lives and live them out, so He offers what I like to call "a dance of abiding in Him." It's a way of living constantly in tune with God, whatever we are doing. Whether we are reading our Bibles with a cup of coffee in hand, or loading the kiddos into the car, or dancing in the ballet studio, or running errands, we have access to the quiet center of Jesus in us. My prayer is that these retreats refresh and renew your soul, inspiring your heart to get into the habit of abiding in Him.

Before you dig in, I have one challenge for you. This is not a requirement, but if you can, take a moment to strategically set aside something, anything, that will give your soul a break while you work through these thirty days. Is there one thing crowding your heart that you could take a break from in order to give yourself space to navigate these daily retreats? Take a moment to ask the Lord what that could be for you. Scribble down in the margins of this page the following sentence: "I'm taking a break from _____." I realize some things that are bogging down your heart can't be eliminated, like the laundry! I'm trying to visualize my home full of three boys and a hubby and what it would look like if I took a break from the laundry for a month. Oh dear! While it would be nice, I know that's probably not realistic.

So for me, something small that wouldn't affect my whole family would be taking a break from social media, watching the news, a major project that's causing stress, adding activities to my calendar, scrolling on my phone, or trying to keep the house perfect. Something tangible that would allow my heart space to grow in God. That choice is going to look different for each of us, but think about one small way you can create space in your soul for what is going to be a really special journey. Do this in a grace-filled way. Don't beat yourself up if you don't make it the whole thirty days without this thing, whatever it may be. This is kind of like putting a stake in the ground that says you're creating space in your heart to hear God's whispers and experience His love and grace in a fresh way.

Perhaps you're not sure what is weighing down your heart. I really believe the Spirit will reveal whatever that thing is as you journey with Him day by day. So if you can't think of anything right now, or it's too difficult to set aside something right now, just go in grace, day by day with God. He will point out little and big ways you can create more space for Him in your daily life.

Another quick note. As in *Dreaming with God*, each chapter has journaling space with reflection questions and prayers for you to use as you like. You can make a mess of this book! For a garden to see beautiful growth, you must dig in the dirt, get your hands messy, and pull out the weeds. New growth and beauty blossom after the hard work of cultivating the soil. In the same way, as you allow yourself to write, revise, underline, and make notes, God will blossom Spiritual growth and inner beauty in you and help you begin to truly flourish as you meet with Him. Don't be afraid to scribble, dog-ear the pages, or put sticky notes in the book. Make it your own. Let it become a keepsake of your journey with God to which you can refer often. I purposely tried to keep these daily retreats simple. Each day has one main Bible verse to focus on, and others are sprinkled throughout the devotions. Concentrate on that one verse for the day, keep your Bible close, and use the reflection questions and prayers to give God space to whisper to your heart.

While I certainly do not have all the answers, I have been desperate for a deeper, daily connection with God. My prayer is that this book will be a retreat from all the distractions. I hope it will help you stay centered on Christ, realigning your heart to Him so that the pull of God becomes stronger in your life than the pull of all the clutter. Thank you for joining me on this journey of tuning in to God so that we can dance through life with joy and focus. I cannot wait to see what He will do in our hearts along the way.

God wants to help steady your heart and wake up your soul to the abundant life He has in store for you (see Ps. 57:7–8). May this book be a springboard into a deeper connection to God as you create space for your heart to get back to dancing in step with Him. The joy and freedom that will come from this daily, behind-the-scenes connection between you and God will create the most beautiful blossoming in your life.

DAY 1

Start Fresh

> Be encouraged that today begins a journey of slowing down,
> savoring Scripture, and drawing closer to God. He wants
> to start something new in you. He has more joy, more life,
> more freedom, and more peace for you. He has treasures
> and jewels for your heart along this journey. Expect new-
> ness of life. Expect a deeper sense of being loved by Him.
> Expect delight.

Behold, I am doing a new thing;
now it springs forth, do you not perceive it?
I will make a way in the wilderness
and rivers in the desert.

ISAIAH 43:19 ESV

STARTING FRESH BEGINS TODAY. It's an invitation to
start over. It's giving ourselves permission to acknowledge that the way we are currently living may be what I like

to call "gunky." We are too cluttered in our hearts and minds, too busy doing instead of being, and too caught up in feeling as though we are missing something better. Something deeper. Something more life-giving. Today let's simply focus on what it means to start fresh.

A flourishing garden is gorgeous, right? It's tended well, it's nourished, it's growing and thriving, it's free of weeds, it's tidy, it's orderly, and it's blooming. Somebody has been working really hard behind the scenes to prepare and refresh the soil, pull the weeds, and carefully place the plants and make sure they are getting all the sun, water, and nourishment they need. A garden is also a process—quite a process. It starts small with a blank canvas of soil, then takes time and seasons to grow. As it thrives, it has to be pruned for new growth to begin. A flourishing garden is a beautiful picture of what God wants for His daughters' hearts.

Maybe the garden of your heart feels more like a mess than a lovely oasis. Just as we talked about in the introduction, perhaps you feel tangled up inside—dry, spiritually bogged down, and mentally and emotionally fatigued. The way to begin refreshing the garden of our hearts is simply by acknowledging that we are starting fresh. By pausing and noting that we are ready to live differently. And thank goodness we have a God who is an expert on making things new. In Revelation 21:5, God declares, "Behold, I am making all things new" (ESV).

Daughter of Christ, that includes you. God knows where you're at and where you've been. He knows what you're feeling. He knows what things are bogging down your heart, soul, and mind and creating havoc within you. He wants to refresh you. He wants to still the tension inside of you and bring you closer to His heart so you can flourish. I love Psalm 107:29–31. Take a look at it here:

> He stilled the storm to a whisper;
> the waves of the sea were hushed.
> They were glad when it grew calm,
> and he guided them to their desired haven.
> Let them give thanks to the Lord for his unfailing
> love. (NIV)

God has the power to still the havoc you feel in your heart to a whisper. He has the power to calm you and guide you to the safe harbor of His presence and grace. He wants to be your haven. From that haven is where your life will begin to bloom. This fresh start today is the beginning of new buds of growth for your heart and your life as you press into the Lord. It's the beginning of something new. So let your hope rise up today. Get excited and feel the hope of a fresh start.

In today's main verse from Isaiah, God declares He is doing something new. The book of Isaiah points out the hope of restoration we have in Christ. Of course, we have the hope of eternal renewal as we get to live forever with God one day. But God is even sweeter. He wants to restore us in this earth-life too. According to Isaiah 43:19, God is doing something new in your life, in my life, and maybe we don't even perceive it. Maybe we can't feel it. Maybe we wonder where He went. Maybe we feel so spiritually dry that we've lost hope and don't feel like we are flourishing. God declares that He can make a way in the wilderness and rivers in the desert.

Think about a wilderness for a moment. The word *wilderness* makes me picture an uncared-for mass of land filled with wild, looming creatures. It sounds kind of scary to me! Now think of a desert. A desert lacks any sign of water. Walking through a desert sounds exhausting. It's hot and almost lifeless. God takes these two places of difficulty and offers hope. He can make a way in the wilderness and a river in the desert. Can you imagine walking through a wilderness, fearful and alone, and suddenly coming up to a clearing? Visualize a lush and beautifully tended path inviting you to a way out. Or imagine walking for days in a parched desert and suddenly catching a glimmer of sparkling water up ahead. As you get closer, you see a never-ending river extending from the east to the west.

God offers a way, a clearing, a lush and beautifully tended path toward relief from the wilderness or desert areas of our lives. A way out of what feels messy in our lives. A way that's ultimately His way. He provides a river that extends across our path, where we can find all the refreshment we need to keep journeying. He is the Way (see John 14:6). He offers this both eternally and here on earth today. This is what starting fresh is about—discovering God along our journey. It's about acknowledging we've been in a wilderness of the heart or a desert of the soul as we've been battling through busyness or distractions or a general feeling of being overwhelmed and seeing that He's the way and He's providing a river of spiritual nourishment as we draw closer to Him.

I encourage you to scribble down some ways you've felt like you've been in the wilderness or desert lately. Acknowledge that it's good and beautiful to be made new and that God always has a fresh start for you. Every single day. Today, tomorrow, and next week. What grace! Lamentations 3:22–23 says,

The steadfast love of the LORD never ceases;
his mercies never come to an end;
they are new every morning;
great is your faithfulness. (ESV)

I typically get the "start fresh" itch right after Christmas—in that week between Christmas and New Year's. I write down ways I want to do things different, things that have been working and things I want to change. God and I do this dance of looking at the garden of my life and heart and seeing what needs to go and what needs to be nurtured. It's fun to reflect, to dig in, and to seek His wisdom for how I can flourish more in my life. All gung ho when New Year's Day comes, I begin to live out these new grace-filled goals the best I can with His help. We get into a rhythm and things are going great for a while.

But often, around March, I lose my rhythm. Somewhere between starting fresh and trying new ways of living in His grace, I start striving. I get busy. I get cluttered in my soul. Life happens. My calendar gets full. But oh His grace! His beautiful invitation to start fresh, to dance in the rhythms of His grace, is there every day when I wake up. I have an *oh yes!* moment. I don't have to do life by myself. I don't have to strive, stress, and strategize. I don't have to walk or dance alone through the wilderness or desert of life. God is always near. He always offers a way through life, down to the everyday steps I take. He always offers the river of His company to refresh me for the journey. And He offers these things to you as well—every day. He extends a fresh start to you this moment. Lay aside the past. Lay aside what's not working. Acknowledge that you want the newness of life He offers. And in His faithful way, He will guide you to the haven of joy and abundant life He has for you. God is the God of fresh starts, and today begins *your* fresh start.

GARDEN MOMENTS
for Your Soul

In what ways are you craving a fresh start today?

....

....

....

....

....

What are you laying aside in your life that you recognize is not working or fueling the abundant life you long for?

....

....

....

....

....

Which verses stand out as you look toward newness of life?

....

....

....

....

....

....

....

....

· · · · · · · · · · **Pray** · · · · · · · · · ·

God, You are the God of new life and fresh starts. Thank You for offering me new life eternally but also new life right here, right now. You know me, and You know just how I feel. You know what gunk has been crowding my heart and how I've been living more in a frantic mode than an abundant-life mode. Thank You for delighting in me and restoring me. Every day can be a fresh start with You; by Your grace I can live a life that flourishes. Here are all the things I'm laying aside (list those things) and here are all the ways I long to flourish (list those things). I invite You to begin something new in me today. Thank You for loving me so personally. Thank You for Your offer of abundant life both eternally and now.

DAY 2

Spring for Your Heart

> *God is the One who will do the transforming in your heart. You don't have to transform yourself. He is the One who will bring spring to your heart. Today allow your heart to soak in His presence, trusting Him with the transformation you long for.*

God, you are my God; I eagerly seek you;
I thirst for you;
my body faints for you
in a land that is dry, desolate, and without water.

———

PSALM 63:1

WHEN HINTS OF SPRING are beginning to bloom outside, something inside us often longs to bloom as well. God designed us to want to grow spiritually. Something inside us wants to deepen our roots in His Word, wants to flourish as

His daughters, wants to thrive in the roles He's established for us, wants to love and live well, and wants to grow in His grace. But as you and I both know, sometimes we feel stuck. Instead of growing, we feel like we're wilting a bit. Instead of thriving, we feel like we're trapped in busy mode. Instead of blooming, we feel like we're just going through the motions. God loves to blossom spring in our hearts. "I will give you a new heart and put a new spirit within you; I will remove your heart of stone and give you a heart of flesh" (Ezek. 36:26). He is the One who loves to bring our hearts fresh hope, unveil within us a newness, delight us with His nearness and love, uproot the gunk in our hearts that's suppressing our joy, and bring a beauty and light to our hearts like nothing else in the world can bring. And He's the One who puts that desire for transformation inside us. Take a look at Philippians 2:13: "For it is God who works in you, both to will and to work for his good pleasure" (ESV). God's Spirit is moving in each of us to help us want His will and to work for His good pleasure. That desire for change or transformation inside you is a beautiful gift from God because it will lead to His best for you.

But here's the sweet thing: we don't have to manufacture spring in our hearts. We don't have to force the blooming. God is the One who does the growing, transforming, and flourishing. "We all, with unveiled faces, are looking as in a mirror at the glory of the Lord and are being transformed into the same image from glory to glory; this is from the Lord who is the Spirit" (2 Cor. 3:18). By His grace and love, He nurtures the soil of our hearts as we lean on Him. He prepares our hearts for growth, He digs deep in our souls to encourage us, and He develops the fruit in our character—He is the Master

Gardener of your heart and soul. How precious is that? How sweet that the big God of the universe delights in tending your heart and soul. Psalm 63:1 says, "You, God, are my God" (NIV). He's *my* God. He's *your* God. He's *our* God. And the one true God wants to work in our hearts so we can experience all He intended for us when He created us. He doesn't want us to miss out on the beauty, growth, and blossoming He has for us. He wants to cultivate our souls. He's a master at it.

May your spring-hungry heart remember that God is the Master Gardener of your heart, which He delights in nurturing so that it blossoms, flourishes, and thrives. Psalm 63:1 goes on to say, "Earnestly I seek you; I thirst for you, my whole being longs for you, in a dry and parched land where there is no water." This desire for spiritual growth comes when we feel parched and dry. We feel thirsty for more of God. And deep down we know He is the answer. As the psalmist continues in Psalm 63, he unpacks something beautiful that results from his eagerly seeking God in his thirst: satisfaction.

> So I gaze on you in the sanctuary
> to see your strength and your glory.
>
> My lips will glorify you
> because your faithful love is better than life.
> So I will bless you as long as I live;
> at your name, I will lift up my hands.
> You satisfy me as with rich food;
> my mouth will praise you with joyful lips.
> (Ps. 63:2–5)

As he gazed on God, his soul grew satisfied. I believe as we gaze on God in our spiritual dryness and our longing for spring for our hearts, He satisfies us. He satisfies our longing for change. He satisfies our longing to be filled.

Be encouraged today that He delights in nurturing your heart and soul; He is at work in you to bring new life and new growth in you for your good and His glory. He is using the dryness you may feel in your heart to lead you to spring for your heart. Take a look at one last verse today: "I am sure of this, that he who started a good work in you will carry it on to completion until the day of Christ Jesus" (Phil. 1:6). God has started something in you, and He's not going to stop transforming your heart until His good work is complete—until the day of Christ Jesus.

God is on a mission to bring spring to your heart throughout your lifetime. He will never stop the work of gardening your precious heart. You can trust Him with that work. You can trust Him to keep your heart blossoming into all that He wants it to be. You can trust Him fully. He doesn't promise us that every single season of our lives will be spring. He will walk us through spiritual drought, but we can know that He will always be working toward spring for our hearts.

GARDEN MOMENTS
for Your Soul

In what ways have your heart and soul felt dry in this season?

....

....

....

....

....

....

....

How have you tried to transform your own heart?

....

....

....

....

....

....

How does it encourage you today to remember that you do not have to do the transforming?

....

....

....

....

....

....

....

· · · · · · · · · · **Pray** · · · · · · · · ·

Lord, thank You for being the Master Gardener of my heart. Here are the ways I feel thirsty to know You deeper and to grow spiritually. (List those things here.) Thank You for allowing me to rely on You when I feel thirsty. You satisfy my heart and soul. Thank You for doing the transforming work in my heart. Here I am, Lord—transform me. Blossom spring within me as I gaze on You.

DAY 3

Retreat with Jesus

> *Daughter of Christ, shed all the things that are tangling you up inside, and come and sit at the Son's feet. He's with you. He's here. He's inviting you to get some much-needed rest for your weary soul. Will you join Him now?*

Come to me, all you who are weary and burdened,
and I will give you rest. Take my yoke upon you
and learn from me, for I am gentle and humble
in heart, and you will find rest for your souls.
For my yoke is easy and my burden is light.

MATTHEW 11:28–30 NIV

How is your soul?
Our souls get crowded with worry, overloaded with
the items on our to-do lists, and depleted from all that we
carry. Maybe your heart and soul feel a bit broken inside,

33

bogged down. Maybe when you sat down today with this book, you were hoping for an instantaneous renewal.

I don't doubt that God could renew our hearts in an instant, but I have a feeling He wants us to know that the renewal—the wholeness, the undoing of busyness, the undoing of stress, the undoing of feeling overwhelmed, the getting back to stillness, the realignment of our hearts back into the strong fortress of God's loving embrace—is going to take time. It's going to be a slow growing, a slow unfurling of the entanglements of our hearts, a slow transformation. But it's going to be oh so good as we take a step toward rest and retreating with the One who waits for us.

Today's verse is familiar to most of us. It's the go-to verse when we're weary. It's the calming verse when we need rest. So again and again, we return to it. Let's take a closer look as we focus on this theme of retreating with Jesus.

Jesus modeled a pattern of retreating when He dedicated moments away from His busy life to spend time alone with the Father.

> And rising very early in the morning, while it was still dark, he departed and went out to a desolate place, and there he prayed. (Mark 1:35 ESV)

> But Jesus often withdrew to lonely places and prayed. (Luke 5:16 NIV)

> In these days he went out to the mountain to pray, and all night he continued in prayer to God. (Luke 6:12 ESV)

Jesus had a mission to save people. The common thread laced throughout His ministry was that He retreated from the activity and the doing to pray and be alone with God. Repeatedly, we see in Scripture how Jesus spent time in solitude, silence, and prayer. I love this moment in Mark, when Jesus recognizes His disciples' busyness and weariness and invites them to pull over and simply be with Him and rest:

Then, because so many people were coming and going that they did not even have a chance to eat, he said to them, "Come with me by yourselves to a quiet place and get some rest." (Mark 6:31 NIV)

Jesus is asking us to simply come to Him. To set aside the constant busyness and step toward Him to be with Him. Because He created us, He knows we are designed for solitude, silence, and time with Him. And He knows the best refreshment for our weary souls is Himself. His pattern of living was to retreat and pray. Think of all Jesus gained during those sacred, quiet moments with His Father. As He pressed into His Father's company, God strengthened Him for His mission, gave Him instructions and guidance, comforted Him in His struggles, and encouraged Him. The Father's company was Jesus's go-to place for refueling. The Father's company was Jesus's safe haven. So back and forth He went, always knowing that it was in that place that Jesus could find everything He needed for His mission and His life. According to John 17, Jesus prayed for Himself, His disciples, and all believers (that includes me and you!). Jesus shows us that prayer is vital to our lives, our mission, and His great purposes. Retreating with God and prayer go hand in hand. We find our fuel for life when we get alone with God, pray, and open ourselves up to Him.

So what if starting today, every time we feel weary, we pause and take that step toward Him and pray? *The Message* version of Matthew 11:28–30 paints a beautiful picture of what it looks like to retreat with Jesus and shows what we gain as we get alone with Him.

Are you tired? Worn out? Burned out on religion? Come to me. Get away with me and you'll recover your life. I'll show you how to take a real rest. Walk with me and work with me—watch how I do it. Learn the unforced rhythms of grace. I won't lay anything heavy or ill-fitting on you. Keep company with me and you'll learn to live freely and lightly. (Matt. 11:28–30 Message)

As we get alone with God, we will recover our lives. Maybe our lives feel a little caddywonk, and we are ready to let God get us back on our feet. He will gladly help us in that. We will find real rest—not the fake kind the world offers, but real, true, genuine, deep soul rest. We will discover that we can keep that closeness with God as we go back into our lives, walking and dancing in step with His lighter rhythms of grace. As we keep company with Him, we will learn to live more freely and simply. Jesus has a way of nurturing His people so they can go out and live with a deeply rooted peace that only He can offer.

He knows about all those things on your heart. He wants to meet you in those things. He wants to care for you and tend to your heart's deepest needs. He wants you to know He is able to replenish your busy heart and overwhelmed soul. He can put your heart back into alignment with His. He will put you back together again. The first step is simply coming to Him. He promises rest. He promises lightness. It's coming, dear one.

Not too long ago, my youngest son broke his arm, and we were both so excited to get his cast taken off after the prescribed amount of time. Maybe we were expecting more of a normal looking arm, but when the cast came off, his fragile arm was stiff, thin, red, peeling, and weak. With tears in his eyes, he looked at me as if to say, "This was not the plan. This is not how it was supposed to look or feel." And I strove to keep my own emotions in check as the doctor informed us of how very careful my son would need to be for the next several months so that he didn't fracture his arm again. The doctor informed us that it was going to take time to build up his muscles and strength again. What my son needed for now was to retreat from activity and to rest. And his crookedy, scaly, frail arm reminded me in that moment of what my heart really needs in my overwhelmed moments: a retreat with Jesus.

I wanted my son to know healing was coming. I wanted him to know that his arm was going to be strong and stable and well soon. I wanted to wrap my assurance all around him and let him know it was all going to turn out okay. We headed home from the doctor's office, and I got Colt situated on the couch with his arm propped up and a blanket over him. After stumbling my way through what I think were hope-filled words to encourage his heart, we turned on *Wild Kratts*, ate some chocolate chip waffles, and sipped on a banana smoothie. He seemed to believe me that all would be well soon.

God wants me to know my heart is going to grow stronger and steadier as I retreat with Him. And He wants you to know that your heart is going to grow stronger and steadier as you retreat with Him too.

It makes me smile to think about the Father lovingly looking down on you and me today, so grateful that we took the step of drawing closer to Him, trusting He is going to make us well soon. He's so glad we're here. So today we can lean in close to God, trusting that healing and wholeness, less stress and busyness, and deeper peace are all coming. But it will take time. And just like I am thoroughly enjoying my son's sweet company for now before he runs off into the world strong, mighty, and free of his broken arm, I know the Father is grateful to have you sitting here in His company today before you are off and running strong, mighty, and free into the world. And just like I want my son to get strong again so he can do all the things he was made to do, the Father wants you to be strong again so you can go and do all the things you were made to do.

This is where it all starts. Simply coming to Him or retreating with Him. Simply pausing all the chaos and sitting with Him. Daughter, He knows all that is on your plate. He knows you cannot stop your life from moving rapidly in all its directions, throw your responsibilities to the wind, and sit in your rocking chair all day with Him. Although, doesn't that sound divine? I'll have some sweet tea with that! But He wants you to know He's always here. He's always available. So keep coming. Come when your heart is full and peaceful. Come when your heart is anxious and tied up in knots. Come in the morning. Come in the evening. Come in the heap of laundry. Come in the messy kitchen. Come in the middle of the ballet studio. Come in the outdoors or indoors. He's waiting. But how sweet that He will never stop waiting to meet your needs. He is constantly waiting to bless your heart with the power of His Word, the depth of His love, and the beauty of His Spirit. Know you can always come to Him and you can always bring Him your mess and overwhelmed heart. He promises rest for your weary soul. Your soul is on its way to wholeness, freedom, grace, and peace. You have found the right place to meet Him. Right here—with Him. To operate well in the busyness, we need to retreat deeply. As you retreat with Jesus, He will enable you to get back to dancing in step with His rhythms of grace. Retreating with Jesus is where your soul finds wellness.

GARDEN MOMENTS
for Your Soul

What things are entangling your heart today?

....

....

....

....

....

....

....

....

What are you bringing to Jesus today?

....

....

....

....

....

How have you been trying to hustle and handle these things on your own?

....

....

....

....

....

· · · · · · · · · · · **Pray** · · · · · · · · · · ·

Jesus, I thank You that I can come to You today and anywhere and anytime. Thank You for Your precious offer of wholeness, peace, healing, and help. Lord, I know You are there, but I can't always seem to sense Your presence and help in my life. I want to run this race strong, mighty, and free, but right now my heart feels overwhelmed, tired, and worried. I get caught up in all the wrong things. I allow the stress and darkness of the world to infiltrate my heart and soul. I want to know

You intimately and experience deeper peace and joy in my life, but all these things are entangling me today. (List those things here.) I give you every entanglement, stress, and worry. I set it all down right here today as I retreat with You. I am asking for Your peace today, knowing that all will be well soon. Keep me on this path with You. Retrain, transform, and heal my heart. Thank You for loving me so tenderly. Thank You for watching over me so sweetly. Thank You for offering to take on my burdens. I want to learn from You how to be in this life, burdens and weariness and all, but with a heart that is steady, free, and strong. Will You show me, Lord? Will You meet me here in these retreats with You? Teach me and make me new, sweet Lord. I am ready to know You deeper, know Your Word better, and live in a new way that brings You glory.

DAY 4

Listen for His Whispers

God wants to speak to you in the quiet moments of your day. He wants to "tell you great and unsearchable things you do not know" (Jer. 33:3 NIV) as you, in faith, step out of the busyness and distractions that have your heart on overload and call to Him for all you need. As you quiet your heart and tune in to Him, His whispers will grow clear.

The LORD was not in the wind. And after the wind an earthquake, but the LORD was not in the earthquake. And after the earthquake a fire, but the LORD was not in the fire. And after the fire the sound of a low whisper. And when Elijah heard it, he wrapped his face in his cloak and went out and stood at the

entrance of the cave. And behold, there came a voice
to him and said, "What are you doing here, Elijah?"

1 KINGS 19:11–13 ESV

GOD WANTS TO BE THE HEARTBEAT of our living. He
wants to keep us right in step with Him as we dance
our dance through life, and He wants to be our constant
guide. But Scripture echoes that God doesn't necessarily
speak loudly, like fireworks or lightning bolts, but in gentle
whispers. In order that we may hear Him, He invites us to
listen intently. That requires quietness, solitude, and alone
time with Him. We gain so much when we slow our pace to
spend time with the One who created us. Today I want to
focus on the beautiful gift of getting to hear His whispers.
Yes, we get to pray and pour out our hearts to the God of
the universe, but what's maybe even more amazing is that
we get to hear from Him. But let's be clear—we're not talking about an audible voice. I know most of us would like to
better understand how we hear God without hearing an audible voice. I understand that dilemma. I'm raising my hand
here, as I often wish I could have something more tangible
to listen for. Today we're going to sit in that tension of not
quite understanding how God speaks or what He "sounds"
like. It makes me think of a dancer. Because the notes are
so soft and subtle, rather than hearing the music, in a way
she's more feeling it. The music takes over her soul and she
can anticipate it even before she hears it because she's so
familiar with it.

As we grow more and more familiar with God, we begin
to understand when we indeed hear His whispers. You know
what I love? I love that God chooses to speak softly, through

the Holy Spirit, because hearing His whispers requires that we scoot up really close to His heart. It requires that we stay close to Him. It requires that we nurture our relationship with Him, protect it from distractions and busyness, and maintain that closeness with Him. He could have chosen to simply hand us our marching orders and send us off on our mission for the day. But instead, He invites us to something much better—connection with Him.

Today's passage from 1 Kings shows us how, in this instance, God spoke softly in a whisper. Maybe Elijah, like most of us, had assumed God would speak in the big, spectacular things, like wind, earthquakes, or fire. How many times have we needed a word from God and began looking for Him to speak in some huge, obvious way? Maybe we wanted guidance for a particular decision, wisdom for our life, or just His affirmation in general, and we felt discouraged that He didn't seem to be speaking. He didn't send some big affirmation. In fact, maybe it seemed as though He was silent.

I love the Lord so much, and so I desire His direction, His approval, His blessing, and His wisdom for my decisions, my path, and everything in between. But oftentimes I become frustrated because I don't see His big stamp of approval in my life. I pray for affirmation and guidance, but my path feels foggy and unclear. I look for His signs of direction, a road map, if you will. His marching orders for me. But what I've learned over time is that what He wants most from me before He sends me out into the world is for me to draw close to Him and listen for His whispers. When I set aside my need to hear from God in a big way and simply draw close to His heart, that direction or clarity I was

so desperately looking for seems to suddenly catch me off
guard in the middle of my everyday moments or right there
in that time with Him. It's like His gentle whispers find
their way to me after I make the choice to be with Him for
no other reason than to know Him and grow familiar with
Him. From that place, He seems to clear the fog with His
Word and presence, and I feel His direction and guidance
over my life again.

I love *The Message* version of Jeremiah 33:3, which says,

> Call to me and I will answer you. I'll tell you marvelous and
> wondrous things that you could never figure out on your
> own.

I tend to lean toward trying to figure out things on my
own instead of coming to God first and listening for His
sweet whispers. I think it's exciting that God wants to whisper
marvelous and wondrous truths, encouragement, peace,
guidance, and wisdom into our hearts throughout our whole
lives. He wants to constantly remind us of the truth of His
Word, the gospel, and that He's always with us (see Isa.
41:10). He wants to encourage us in our dance through life.
He wants to pour peace into our hearts so we can live with
deeply rooted joy and sense that all is well no matter our
circumstances. He wants to guide us and give us wisdom,
His wisdom, so we can dance this life free, full-out, and
abundantly. So He speaks into our lives. And as you and I
grow familiar with His presence, we will begin to recognize
His whispers.

How do we grow familiar with His presence? How do
we know we're hearing from Him? We must keep His Word

at the forefront of our lives. The Word is God's road map, love letter, and instruction manual for our lives. He wants to personally whisper to our souls through His Word. And when we're not sure if we're hearing God's whispers, simply ask. "Ask and it will be given to you; seek and you will find; knock and the door will be opened to you" (Matt. 7:7 NIV). I believe that request from your heart to God's would absolutely delight Him. He would love to make sure you're hearing His whispers. I wish I could plainly describe in a tangible way what hearing from God sounds or feels like, but I think that the mystery of it keeps us seeking Him. And that's ultimately what He wants.

Know today that He wants to speak into your life. He's not hiding from you or trying to make it difficult for you. But hearing from Him does require that you purposely listen. He longs for you to quiet your heart and tune in. That you want to hear from Him, to listen for His gentle whispers over your life, is a beautiful thing. I believe He is going to honor that desire of your heart. "Delight yourself in the LORD, and he will give you the desires of your heart" (Ps. 37:4 ESV). He may speak to you in the quiet moments, when it's just you and God with your Bible open on your lap. He may speak to you as you're scribbling your thoughts to Him in your journal. Or He may speak to you while you're washing the dishes, walking the dog, or running errands. There's no limit to the places, times, or ways He will whisper to you, but know He is whispering over your life. And as you become more and more aware of His nearness and His desire to whisper to you, you will begin to know when He's speaking.

GARDEN MOMENTS
for Your Soul

Which verses today encourage your heart that God is whispering over your life and wants you to hear from Him?

....

....

....

....

In what struggles, circumstances, or situations do you need to hear from God today?

....

....

....

....

How can you tangibly quiet your heart and tune in to God today?

....

....

....

....

Pray

God, I want to listen to Your gentle whispers over my life. I want to hear from You. Thank You for the gift of Your Spirit and that I get to hear from You. Thank You that my desire to hear from You keeps me dependent on You and close to You. Today I long to quiet the noise and busyness and truly tune in to You. Will you show me what that looks like for me personally? What things can I set aside? What noise can I turn off? What busyness can I tune out? What do You have to whisper to me today? Help me make a point of listening for Your sweet whispers every day. Thank You that as I draw closer to You, Your whispers will grow clear. Speak to Your daughter today and every day. I'm ready to listen.

DAY 5

Heart-Space

Daughter of Christ, your heart is precious to God because it's the place where He resides in you. "Don't you know that you yourselves are God's temple and that God's Spirit dwells in your midst?" (1 Cor. 3:16 NIV). And it's the place where He develops you for His kingdom purposes. Your heart needs space to know God and to grow, change, and blossom into all that He desires for you. Daughter, let today be a fresh beginning to create heart-space so that the garden of your life will begin to truly flourish.

Keep your heart with all vigilance,
for from it flow the springs of life.

PROVERBS 4:23 ESV

TODAY WE ARE GOING TO TALK ABOUT this word I may have kind of made up—heart-space. In a day and age when we have access to so much information, so much news,

49

so much social media interaction, so many opportunities, and so much activity in general, it is vital that we guard and tend our hearts so we can stay in tune with God and truly flourish as His daughters.

Proverbs 4:23 is like a go-to verse for heart-space. It's a reminder that guarding our hearts is really important. In fact, the New International Version says, "Above all else, guard your heart, for everything you do flows from it." That astounds me to think about it in that way—above *everything* (to-do lists, deadlines, leisure activities, decisions) guard your heart. And *everything* we do (follow our dreams, raise our kiddos, work, create, accomplish, dance our dance, grow as God's daughters) flows from it. *The Message* version says it this way: "Keep vigilant watch over your heart; *that's* where life starts." And I love this little nugget in the verses following: "Keep your eyes straight ahead; ignore all sideshow distractions. Watch your step, and the road will stretch out smooth before you. Look neither right nor left" (vv. 24–27). Life—full life, abundant life—flows directly from God's heart to our hearts. So we need to be proactive about guarding our hearts. I think this is particularly difficult to do in our day and age when we have so much before us, but I believe it's possible because nothing is impossible with God (see Luke 1:37). Oftentimes the first step to guarding our hearts is simply being aware that we need to tend them. And that's what today is about—being aware of the treasure and gift of our hearts and vigilantly taking care to guard and tend them.

Your precious heart is the base from which everything you do in life stems. It's your root system, in a way. As I said before, your heart is where God lives. It needs space. Space to grow, to listen to God's whispers, to make room for God's Word to take root, and to guard us from unnecessary stress and anxiety. It makes me think of a garden and how the plants need room to grow. Each plant needs to receive the right amount of nutrients in its root system in order to flourish. If the plants are crowded too close together, they miss some nutrients and do not thrive. They might survive, but they aren't all they could be. In the same way, we can survive with a crowded heart, but we won't flourish and we will miss out on the beauty of God's best for us.

Anything and everything can crowd and deplete a gal's heart. It could be lies she's believed about herself, insecurities that have taken her heart captive, busyness that seems to beckon her to never stop, news that makes her feel fearful or not enough, worries she can't seem to let go of, unhealthy habits that cause her to leave God out. I wish we could sit across from each other over coffee and talk about heart-space and determine what exactly is causing your heart to feel crowded. While I can't be there in person, I hope to offer you encouragement today that it's good and precious to take care of your heart—to tend, protect, and guard it from things that deplete it. You can take care of your heart with the Lord's help simply by beginning that conversation with Him. Ask Him what's crowding your heart and what heart-space would look like for you in a practical sense. God can rejuvenate us when we give ourselves space from the things that are depleting our hearts. We need instead to give God room to shower our hearts with His love. We need space to spend time with Him, space to grow in Him, and space to rest in Him. When we allow this heart-space, our lives begin to flourish and blossom.

Being a mama of three young sons, I have become ultra aware of guarding their hearts. I leap in front of the television when there is a questionable commercial and tell them, "Close your eyes!" I monitor their time playing video games. I notice when we all need to get outside and enjoy God's creation, so I lead them out the door. But sometimes I forget to guard my own heart. I forget that I have to work just as hard to notice when my heart is getting crowded. Maybe it's in different ways that I must guard my heart, but it's just as important that I guard this wellspring of life. In Philippians 4:8, Paul implores us to fill our hearts with "whatever is true, whatever is honorable, whatever is just, whatever is pure, whatever is lovely, whatever is commendable, if there is any excellence, if there is anything worthy of praise, think about these things" (ESV). This verse can be a beautiful and life-giving filter for what we allow into our heart-space.

Recently I was watching my youngest practice a dance for his school talent show. Seeing the mamas try to get forty first graders to space out adequately was simply cute and funny. The kiddos held out their little arms and made sure they had enough space to perform their hip-hop routine and dance full-out. And my little guy did just that. He busted out dancing with all his hip-hop swagger (which he did not get from his ballerina mama).

What a sweet picture of what happens in our dance of life when we give ourselves heart-space. When we guard our hearts and tend them well, we flourish and dance full-out, with God's help, grace, and guidance. When we protect our hearts and give them space to know God intimately, we begin to radiate from within. "Those who look to him are radiant" (Ps. 34:5 NIV). Who doesn't want that kind of glow?

I challenge you today to vigilantly guard your heart. This word *vigilantly* means to be "keenly watchful to detect danger; ever awake and alert."[1] Think about what it would look like for you to be *keenly watchful*, *ever awake*, and *alert* about what's crowding your sweet heart. That heart of yours is gold. It was uniquely shaped and formed (see Ps. 139:13–16). It's where everything in your life stems from. It's worth guarding. It's worth tending. Let God invade your heart-space.

GARDEN MOMENTS
for Your Soul

What things come to mind as you think about what is crowding your heart?

....

....

....

....

....

....

....

....

What are some practical ways you can better tend your heart with God's grace and help?

....

....

....

....

....

....

....

· · · · · · · · · · *Pray* · · · · · · · · · ·

Lord, thank You for bringing my attention to this call to guard my heart. Thank You for waking me up to the importance of tending this space in which You reside. Lord, You know how my heart has been crowded and overly full. You know exactly how I need to create heart-space. You know how I can better guard and tend my heart. Will You guide me in this today? Thank You for being the One who helps me in all things. "I lift up my eyes to the hills. From where does my help come? My help comes from the LORD, who made heaven and earth" (Ps. 121:1–2 ESV). I pray that You would create heart-space within me that reflects everything good and beautiful that comes from You. I give You my heart, and I ask You to reign in it fully. I ask You to ultimately be the keeper of my heart.

DAY 6

Be Rooted

God created you to live deeply rooted in His love, grace, and truth. As you find your footing as a daughter of Christ, buds of new life will begin to spring forth in you. As you deepen your roots in God, He will nurture your faith and you will become grounded in new ways.

Let your roots grow down into him, and let
your lives be built on him. Then your faith
will grow strong in the truth you were taught,
and you will overflow with thankfulness.

COLOSSIANS 2:7 NLT

TODAY WE ARE GOING TO TALK ABOUT our relationship with Christ and how everything we dream of becoming or doing in life stems from being rooted in Him. Being rooted in God is something between you and God—hidden from the world and unseen. God has special works laid out for you: "For we are God's handiwork, created in Christ Jesus to do good works, which God prepared in advance for us to do" (Eph. 2:10 NIV). He wants abundant life for you: "The thief comes only to steal and kill and destroy; I have come that they may have life, and have it to the full" (John 10:10 NIV). And the way we dance in those good works and experience this abundant life He offers is to be rooted in Him.

In our verse for the day, Paul is imploring believers to keep growing in spiritual maturity. He implies that they are constantly growing and learning. I think it's beautiful for you and me to remember that we too are constantly growing and learning, and that God is always maturing us spiritually as we navigate life with Him. But the sweet part is that while our growing may feel messy at times and very much a process, we can know our roots are always in Christ. He never changes. "He is the same yesterday, today, and forever" (Heb. 13:8 CEV).

We can root ourselves in Him every single day by acknowledging Him as Lord of our lives and simply desiring to center our lives on Him. We stay rooted in Him by prioritizing our relationship with Him, reading His Word, and aiming to know Him and do life with Him. Staying rooted in Him isn't a formula or a program or a particular reading plan. As we allow His Spirit to nudge us when we're maybe a little more rooted in the world than in Him, we learn to return to Him over and over again as our strong foundation. It's this dance of grace through which we deepen our roots in Him.

I love this image in Jeremiah 17:7–8 in regard to being rooted in Him:

Blessed is the man who trusts in the LORD,
   whose trust is the LORD.
He is like a tree planted by water,
   that sends out its roots by the stream,
and does not fear when heat comes,
   for its leaves remain green,
and is not anxious in the year of drought,
   for it does not cease to bear fruit. (ESV)

These verses make "being rooted" practical. Rootedness blesses us. Rootedness in God makes us joyful, happy, free, content, set apart! I love that. A person rooted in God also *trusts* in the Lord. She trusts God with her life. And because of that trust in Him (both for eternity and for abundant life on earth), she is like a tree planted by water. A tree planted by water is nourished, strong, steady, and thriving because its roots receive all they need from the water. The tree isn't worried about harsh conditions because it's so rooted. It will always remain green and bear fruit. Daughter of Christ, your life is designed to bear fruit. You are designed to be rooted in God so that He can keep you nourished, strong, steady, and thriving. You don't have to do more or be more to be rooted. I think being rooted is more about the posture of your heart and trusting God with everything. It means you surrender to the One who gardens your life. As you grow in your faith and find your footing in Christ, He is growing your roots deeper and deeper in Him. And from that rootedness, your heart and life will flourish into all the beauty He created them to be.

My favorite tree is one I pass by nearly every day in our neighborhood. I believe it's a pear tree, and from what I understand, pear trees are not the most stable, but they are stunning and beautiful. I love watching the tree evolve through the seasons, and I particularly enjoy the white blossoms that bud in the spring. This tree remains sturdy and strong throughout every season. Whether my pup Shaka and I are power walking in the gusty, cold winds of winter or enjoying a warm, sunny day, the tree does its thing. It loses its leaves in the fall, remains strong through the winter, hints buds of spring and busts out in color and beauty as the weather warms—and it remains strong and thriving throughout the summer days. Again and again it cycles through its patterns, and over and over I'm reminded that a gal who trusts in the Lord is just like that beautiful, blossoming tree. She's doing her thing, rooting herself in God and His Word, dancing her dance with the Lord. She's growing in seasons, blossoming, and remaining strong and thriving because of the Lord. Whether she's at the beginning of her journey, somewhere in the messy middle, or flourishing in more seasoned years, she truly begins to sparkle when she finds her rootedness in God.

Being rooted starts with hidden moments with God and nurturing your relationship with Him. It's the behind-the-scenes dance of meeting with Him, praying, listening for His whispers, and allowing Him to lead your life. Rootedness is hidden, just like the roots of a tree. And you know what I believe? I believe those hidden moments of tending your spiritual roots in God will become your favorite moments. When you meet with God and discover the goodness He has for you, what could easily be perceived as a chore or duty becomes a delight. And before you know it, you will begin to crave those hidden moments with Him. As He nurtures your spiritual roots, ultimately He draws you closer to Him.

And that's where your delight, joy, and peace stem from. Be rooted in God and discover the richness of the strongest foundation, which is God Himself.

GARDEN MOMENTS
for Your Soul

How are your spiritual roots? Does it feel like you're nourished and thriving or dry and just surviving?

....

....

....

....

....

What would it look like, practically speaking, for you to nurture your spiritual roots?

....

....

....

....

....

What challenges you to stay rooted in God?

....

....

....

....

....

....

....

· · · · · · · · · · **Pray** · · · · · · · · · ·

Lord, I long to be rooted in You. I am weary of feeling dry and wobbly. I need You as my strong foundation. Show me how to nurture my spiritual roots so that I live nourished and thriving instead of dry and just surviving. Allow my heart to be deeply rooted in Your beautiful Word. Steady my heart, mind, and soul in the well of Your life-giving Word. Allow my heart to flourish like a strong, secure, blossoming tree as I grow my roots in You and Your Word. Help me delight in meeting with You, conversing with You, and discovering new things in Your Word. Help me remember that it's during these hidden moments with You when my spiritual roots grow deeper. Thank You for loving me so personally and for caring about the welfare of my heart, mind, and soul. "Great is the Lord, *who delights in the welfare of his servant!" (Ps. 35:27 ESV).*

Find Strength

The world out there is busy and full. You are working hard in your realm of influence, doing all you were made to do. Come back to the Lord anytime you need refreshing. Find strength in the quiet moments with Him so that you go back to your work renewed, stronger, and energized.

Do you not know?
Have you not heard?
The LORD is the everlasting God,
the Creator of the whole earth.
He never becomes faint or weary;
there is no limit to his understanding.
He gives strength to the faint
and strengthens the powerless.
Youths may become faint and weary,
and young men stumble and fall,
but those who trust in the LORD
will renew their strength;

they will soar on wings like eagles;
they will run and not become weary,
they will walk and not faint.

ISAIAH 40:28–31

TODAY WE ARE GOING TO TALK ABOUT this back and forth-ness that God designed us for—going out and doing the things He's called us to do and then returning to Him to find the strength we need to go out again. It's a dance, and what I love is that it keeps us fueled up and close to our Maker's heart.

Today's verse from Isaiah is a great reminder that we find our strength in God. I love the prophet's questions that begin these beautiful verses: "Do you not know? Have you not heard?" He's getting our attention. He's excited for the truth he is about to lay out. He wants to make sure we are paying full attention. He goes on to describe our strong God: "Everlasting God, the Creator of the whole earth. He never becomes faint or weary; there is no limit to his understanding. He gives strength to the faint and strengthens the powerless." Your weariness is not too exhausting for Him. He understands every angle of your weariness because He created you and knows you. He will gladly strengthen you.

The prophet goes on to declare that "those who trust in the LORD will renew their strength." There's that word *trust* again that we discussed in previous chapters. Trust seems to be the one common denominator for our themes of flourishing that we've been talking about. Not only will we find strength, the prophet says, but "[we] will soar on wings like eagles; [we] will run and not become weary." Soar? Run? Yes! As we learn this dance of going out and returning to God

64

to find strength again, our living will feel less like burnout and more like soaring and running.

Sometimes I think I could love this Christian life more and live it with more strength and freedom if I lived far out in the middle of nowhere. Just me, my sweet hubby, my children, and, well, I would like to add all my family members too. Just us and our pup. Living right by a river with big, wide-open spaces. Daily walks through the wildflowers would be my top priority. Horses would be a must. We wouldn't need cell phones because we would all be right there together, but we might have Netflix so we could enjoy our favorite shows together. Life would be simple. Quieter. More peaceful. Or so I think.

Spiritually, sometimes I wish I could live in a bubble too. I wish God would let me live happily ever after, without having to really engage in the world too much. I find myself wanting to separate from the world. But as we talked about earlier, Jesus's pattern during His public ministry was quite different from my little dream of living in the country and separating from the world. He went back and forth. Before the busyness of the day took over, He met with His Father and prayed. But then He entered the busyness. After full days of loving on people and meeting their needs, He pulled away for a bit to rest and pray. And when the crowds grew big and His heart became weary, He pulled away on a boat all by Himself to be with the One who strengthened Him. There was this back and forth-ness to His ministry. To work, then back to the Father. Once He found strength in His Father, He went out again to His work.

I tend to think that if I could just stay with the Father all day for my whole life, then I would be better off. I could live without busyness, stress, distractions, and worry. God and I would dance our dance in our own little world, and my heart would overflow with peace and joy. I would pull away and shut myself off from the world. Would life really be easier?

Maybe you feel the same way. Maybe you wish you could shut off the world completely and live your life in peace. Maybe you wish you didn't have to go out into the world and do and be what God has called you to do and be. Maybe you are tired of being tired, so you would rather hole up in a home in the middle of nowhere, just you and the wildflowers.

The state of our world can certainly make us feel like isolating ourselves rather than engaging in the ministries and work our God has set before us. But I encourage us all (me too) to remember that Jesus's life points us to the way He wants us to live. We are called to partner with God through the trials, tests, and stresses. It's a life of retreating with God to find strength again. Our human hearts were not designed to go, go, go all day long. They were made to pull over and rest.

But in the same breath, our human hearts were not made to rest all day long either. They were made to impact, work, do, and be. They were made to love, help, and minister. They were made to create, enjoy, and be passionate. We were made for a dance of work and rest. We work with and for the Father, and we find strength and rest with the Father. He is always there. He constantly helps us in our weariness. Because of God's continuous support, we don't have to rely on our own strength all the time. This back and forth-ness is a dance through which we find our strength to live in this world.

As we enjoy these quiet moments and retreats with God each day, may we remember that we will need to reenter the world. But oh what a joy and gift to have a place (in Him) where we can regain our strength. How beautiful and life-giving that we do not go into the world unequipped. The key is to learn to recognize when we need to retreat and when it's time to return to our work. Remember, He goes into our work with us. So how do you know when it's time to retreat and find strength again? Your heart tells you in all kinds of ways, and the Spirit pursues you. You may feel a restlessness deep in your heart or maybe you experience an overall feeling of fatigue. Perhaps you feel burned-out or simply too busy.

God designed our hearts to alert us when they're spiritually thirsty. Just like how it is obvious when flowers need watering because they look dry and limp, our hearts give us signals when they're dry and need spiritual watering. We were made for God, and when we do not get our hearts close to Him, they become thirsty. We can only satisfy our thirst through God. I have mentioned before how we tend to keep going, to keep pushing, and to keep in step with the world. But we know this dance, and we know the world is not the place to find strength. So, covered in grace, we try again—this time landing in the loving arms of God. We remember again that He is the place where we find strength and renewal.

Daughter of Christ, know that while you were made for eternity in heaven, you were also created for good works on earth. The One who made the world resides in you, helping you to live in it but at the very same moment be separated from it. He who made the world lives in you so that you can dance this dance in the world, remembering He is your source of strength.

God wants to use you in this world. He wants to bring His light to your sphere of influence. He needs you to be in the world loving others and shining bright for Him. Don't back away from that. Know that in Him you will find the strength to keep going out into the world, to keep showing up, and to keep dancing this life for His glory. When you feel your heart burning out, when you feel fatigue and weariness setting in, find your strength again in Him. This is your dance. You go out, and then you return to Him for strength. You go out again, and then you return to Him for strength again. He becomes the foundation of your life. And the dance becomes a joy because you always know where to find your strength.

GARDEN MOMENTS
for Your Soul

In what ways have you felt burned-out from your work, whatever that work may be?

....

....

....

....

....

How do you feel encouraged that God wants to be the One to strengthen you?

....

....

....

....

....

How do you know when you need to retreat to the Lord and find your strength in Him?

....

....

....

....

....

· · · · · · · · · · **Pray** · · · · · · · · ·

Lord, thank You for reminding me that You have good works for me to do and, at the very same time, letting me know I can always return to You for strength. Give me a new passion and joy as I go about my work in this world, knowing that the moment I get weary, You are there waiting to build up my strength again. Thank You for the example of Your earth-life. Thank You for giving us a pattern, a model, and steps to follow of this working and retreating dance. Sometimes I get weary, Lord, so change my perspective to see that You are pleased when I go into the world to do the work You have given me, operating out of a strength that comes only from You. And thank You for welcoming me back the moment I need strength again. Thank You that I was made to depend on You, Jesus.

DAY 8

Prune

> *God is doing flourishing work in you. He's budding new life and new growth from within your beautiful heart. But oftentimes, before new growth appears, He prunes. He cuts away the things that are entangling your heart so that new life can bud and blossom. Today lean into His pruning process. Know that the pruning is producing true beauty.*

I am the true vine, and my Father is the gardener.
Every branch in me that does not produce fruit
he removes, and he prunes every branch that produces fruit so that it will produce more fruit.

JOHN 15:1–2

A S YOU MEET WITH GOD, savor Scripture in a fresh way. Curl up close to His heart. He is going to point out things in your heart and life that are keeping you from flourishing as His daughter.

Now, we talked about this somewhat in the chapter "Heart-Space," but today we are going to talk more specifically about the unnecessary things that can clutter our spiritual lives and how God prunes them to bear spiritual fruit within us.

I absolutely love the imagery Jesus uses in John 15 of how He is the true vine, the Father is the gardener, and we, God's daughters, are the branches. This is a picture of connectedness—that as we go about our lives, we are constantly connected, through Jesus, to God. But as the passage goes on, it shows us that as God sees fit, He does some pruning work because there are some things that can negatively affect our connectedness to Him. When I think of pruning, I think of pruning rosebushes. We cut back the branches even though they look healthy and vibrant because we know that cutting them back allows them to bloom even more beautifully in the future. Cutting them back protects them from getting too big, which would cause the stems to be weighed down and the bushes to be visually unappealing. Cutting them back keeps them in a cycle of beauty. And so we prune. In the same way, Jesus talks about pruning our spiritual lives. He points out that the Father removes branches that are not bearing fruit and prunes ones that are so that they can bear even more fruit. I've experienced this spiritual pruning in my life in numerous ways, but most times it involves cutting out something that's crowding my heart. It feels like a little nudge from God to push aside some distractions, lay down some worries, or reprioritize my relationship with Him. Take a look at this little gem in John 15:16:

> You did not choose me, but I chose you and appointed you
> so that you might go and bear fruit. (NIV)

God chose you and appointed you to bear fruit. He wants your life to flourish, blossom, and be effective for His kingdom and your good. This points to God's sweetness and loving heart. He's not a taskmaster; He's a loving Gardener. He's tender and kind. He's personal and gentle. He wants your life to blossom into all that He created it to be because He loves you and cares for you (see 1 Pet. 5:7). And for you to flourish, He must point out the things in your heart that are keeping you from bearing fruit.

I love this invitation to see our lives in this way. I think it's an opportunity for a heart-to-heart conversation with our Master Gardener, a chance to ask Him specifically what needs pruning. This is not an easy or particularly fun process, but if we can see the beauty in it—that after pruning comes fruit-bearing—then I think we will recognize its value.

So while God's pruning us is not fun, it's good to realize we must allow God's pruning hand to continuously have access to our hearts so He can keep them fruitful. And note, He gives us His Spirit to help us navigate through our weaknesses and sins. "In the same way, the Spirit helps us in our weakness. We do not know what we ought to pray for, but the Spirit himself intercedes for us through wordless groans" (Rom. 8:26 NIV). We have a Helper in all things. "You are my help and my deliverer" (Ps. 40:17 NIV). So with those things in mind, let's walk through some of the things God might want to prune in our hearts so we will bear fruit. This process is going to look very different from one gal to the next, but in general, here are some things, entanglements, that God may lead us to cut away (with His help and grace, of course).

Pruning may involve these things:

- an attitude that needs readjusting
- an influence that is negatively affecting us
- an activity that is not life-giving
- something on our schedule or calendar that could free up space for a slower pace
- a sin that is entangling our hearts
- a lie we're believing
- a pressure or expectation that is weighing down our hearts
- a habit that's not life-giving

The common denominator between all these things is that they may be disrupting our connectedness to our Master Gardener. And this God of ours is a jealous God (see Exod. 20:5), which simply means He loves us so much that He doesn't want anything to come between us and Him. He is jealous for our hearts and devotion, and when He sees something disrupting that oneness with Him, He is going to nudge us about it. Also, His thoughts and ways are not like our thoughts and ways (see Isa. 55:8). He can see things in our lives that need to be pruned that we don't see. Some of this stuff, this gunk, may be keeping us from bearing fruit. So He gladly prunes.

As we ask God to show us what needs pruning, His Spirit will guide and prod us in the right direction. Like Isaiah 30:21 says, "Whenever you turn to the right or to the left, your ears will hear this command behind you: 'This is the way. Walk in it.'" As we choose His way, we will reap the benefits of the pruning, which are new life, new growth, and fresh fruit-bearing. That's something to get really excited about! Pruning will not be easy; in fact, it may even hurt. We may feel alone on our journey in that season, but know that it will be worth the work. Through the pruning process, we will not only bear fruit in a new way, but we will hear His whispers of love over us in a profound way as we make room and space for a deeper connection to the Master Gardener.

I think of God as our loving parent. And just like those of us who sometimes have to point out little things that need to go from our children's hearts so their character grows, God lovingly points out what needs pruning in us so that we, too, can mature.

What I want you to see is that as you press into the pruning process, with God's help and grace, you will experience a new season. And it will be oh so good, so worth it. God has more blossoming for you on the other side of pruning.

GARDEN MOMENTS
for Your Soul

Can you describe a pruning season in your life and what good things came out of that season?

....

....

....

....

Take some quiet moments to reflect on what things God might want to prune in your current season.

....

....

....

....

....

....

· · · · · · · · · ·   *Pray*   · · · · · · · · ·

Lord, thank You that You are the Master Gardener. Thank You that we get to be connected to You through Jesus and the Holy Spirit. Lord, I recognize things can disrupt the connectedness between us. Today I open my heart to the ways You may want to do some pruning within me. Will You shed light on those things in my life that are entangling my heart, keeping me from bearing fruit, and disrupting my relationship with You? And will You help me see that Your pruning is for my good and Your glory? Lord, I want to live a fruitful life. I want to blossom into all that You created me to be, but I need Your help, grace, guidance, and wisdom. And I need You constantly, every step of the way. May I see pruning in a new light—as a gift that leads to more life. Thank You for coming to give us life both eternally and abundantly. You are good.

Prune

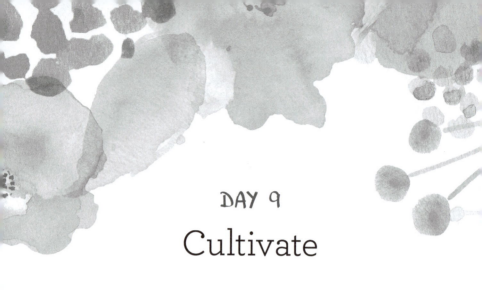

DAY 9

Cultivate

God can cultivate the sweetest contentment in your heart as you take His hand and let Him deck you with wildflowers. As you notice the beauty and divine love lavished on you, you will begin to flourish right where you already are. And as you embrace the life God has given you, you will find everything you always wanted.

Trust in the LORD and do good;
Dwell in the land and cultivate faithfulness.

PSALM 37:3 NASB

TODAY WE ARE GOING TO TALK ABOUT this idea of cultivating our lives. I love some of the definitions of cultivate: "to prepare," "to promote or improve the growth of," "to develop," "to refine," "to foster," and "to devote oneself."[1] What I want us to see is that when we cultivate and fully dig into where God has us, we take on another level of flourishing and beauty. We *improve the growth of our spiritual lives*. As we slow our pace and take time to develop, refine, and foster our right-now life and devote our hearts to the current season, we find deeply rooted contentment. While we still have hopes and dreams for the future, we thrive as we embrace contentment. As Psalm 38:9 tells us, God knows our desires and dreams: "Lord, my every desire is in front of you; my sighing is not hidden from you." But we learn to trust Him with them and with our future as we cultivate our present circumstances. Our human nature is to rush ahead, want the next big thing, or move on to the next season. But as Paul describes in Philippians 4:12, the secret of fostering contentment in our lives is like discovering the key to living joyfully and to thriving versus surviving.

> I know what it is to be in need, and I know what it is to have plenty. I have learned the secret of being content in any and every situation, whether well fed or hungry, whether living in plenty or in want. (Phil. 4:12 NIV)

Notice that Paul had to *learn* contentment. It's not something that came naturally or easily to him. We, too, must learn contentment. But what I want you to see today is that cultivating contentment is a precious secret to living life joyfully and peacefully.

So how do we cultivate contentment? Let's circle back around to our verse for today. This verse is a reminder that, as we cultivate our right-here, right-now lives, more flourishing is inevitable. A deeper sense of God's presence, peace, and love is sewn deeper into our hearts.

Again, it's an invitation to *trust in the Lord*. As we trust in the Lord by digging deep in our current lot and leaving the future to Him, He will develop contentment in us. As we trust in Him and *do good*—do the things He has put in our path today—and *dwell*—be fully invested where He has us—He will cultivate contentment in our hearts.

The last little phrase of Psalm 37:3—"cultivate faithfulness" (NASB)—is translated in many ways in different Bible versions. Take a look at some examples:

"Enjoy safe pasture" (NIV)

"Then you will live safely in the land and prosper" (NLT)

"Befriend faithfulness" (ESV)

"Live securely"

"Feed on faithfulness" (ISV)

This paints a picture of security and thriving as we depend on God's faithfulness. We enjoy safe pasture. And this is the most beautiful place to be—dwelling in God's goodness, not worried or anxious for the future but fully enjoying our right-now life and trusting God to faithfully guide us through each season.

At times we may feel anxious for the upcoming thing, ready to hear from God about the next season, in a hurry for more, better, or different. I pray today that you're encouraged to joyfully dwell in your current season. I pray you're inspired to cultivate contentment where you are and to see that God is lavishing His love on you this very moment and wants you to live freely and lightly (see Matt. 11:28–30). I pray you hear His whispers of love and assurance. He has your future taken care of, so you can fully enjoy and dig deep into where your feet already are. And as you do, I believe you will grow to love where He has you. God is developing, restoring, and transforming you. Dig deep, cultivate, and discover the sweet secret of contentment.

GARDEN MOMENTS
for Your Soul

What future things have been on your mind that are keeping you from fully digging into your current season?

....

....

....

....

What would it look like for you to love and enjoy the beautiful grass under your toes right now?

....

....

....

....

....

Make a list of the things in your right-now season that are good, lovely gifts from above, and reflect on what it would look like to really cultivate those things.

....

....

....

....

....

....

· · · · · · · · · · *Pray* · · · · · · · · · ·

God, thank You for being the tender of my soul and my life. Thank You for Your invitation to cultivate my right-now life and to see that every good gift is from You. Would You help me see this season as good, lovely, and beautiful? Would You help me develop contentment in my heart as I learn to trust You more deeply with my life? Would You help me love and enjoy the precious life You have given me right here and right now? Thank You that You know the desires and dreams of my heart. Help me entrust those things to You and then purposefully and intentionally plant my feet in the present moment and season. I know You have good and sweet things You want to show me and develop in me during this time. Don't let me miss them. Help me slow down and savor what You're doing right here and right now.

Cultivate

DAY 10

Pour Out

Today pour out your heart to God. While "[God] knows the secrets of [your] heart" (Ps. 44:21 ESV), He wants a relationship with you. And a relationship takes conversations—heart-to-heart talks—and listening. As you talk to Him about your burdens, stresses, worries, and concerns (all of it!), you will discover a "peace that surpasses all understanding" (Phil. 4:7).

Trust in him at all times, you people;
pour out your hearts to him,
for God is our refuge.

PSALM 62:8 NIV

TODAY I WANT TO DIVE INTO ANOTHER WAY we can embrace how God turns our wild lament into whirling dance and decks us with wildflowers: pouring out our hearts to Him in prayer. As we do this, He takes us from a state of feeling stressed and anxious to a place of feeling loved and free of our burdens.

God lovingly gathers every concern of our hearts and watches over our lives intently, ready to pick us up the moment we call out to Him. He loves for us to pour out our hearts to Him, and He takes our burdens and gives us an unexplainable peace in return. Psalm 62:8 inspires us to trust Him at all times (good times, hard times, frustrating times, confusing times) because He is our safe refuge.

He cheers us on from the wings of life. He is always right there waiting to sweep us off our feet and carry us. There is something so freeing and beautiful about this process. When we pour out our hearts to God, He pours in His comfort and truth. Our hearts are lighter, and we feel His beautiful presence.

Sometimes pouring out our hearts feels silly, or selfish, or hard. So we keep everything tucked away deep inside instead of reaching for Him. We hate to bother Him with what is going on inside our hearts. Or we know He knows what's going on, so why express it in prayer? Isn't He all-knowing? There is something about the act of pouring it out. It opens the communication lines between us and God. When we pour out our hearts to Him, our relationship grows deeper and sweeter. There is a transaction of trading in our concerns for His peace that happens. Philippians 4:6–7 tells us this: "Do not be anxious about anything, but in everything by prayer and supplication with thanksgiving let your requests be made known to God. And the peace of God, which surpasses all understanding, will guard your hearts and your minds in Christ Jesus" (ESV).

We feel His comfort. We feel His concern. And our trust in Him grows. Our tendency is to keep it all hidden away, but the God of the universe invites us to get specific and detailed. He wants to know what has your heart tangled up in knots, because He wants to untangle it. He wants to know the things that are troubling you, because He wants to hold them so you don't have to. He wants to help you. And He longs for you to tell Him what's in your heart.

He may not fix the situation that very moment; your circumstances probably will not change that instant. But you will feel different. You will know His presence and comfort. Your heart will feel lighter, untangled.

So what's on your heart today? What things are tangling you up inside, weighing heavily on your soul? What are you keeping inside that needs to be poured out to your Father? He longs for you to know that He is constant and present in your life, always cheering you on. He yearns for you to know that He is the safest place for you to pour out your heart. He wants to remove the things that are weighing down your heart and to fill you with His joy. And as you pour out to Him, you will discover His peace filling you up. Pouring out all the things weighing on your heart will make room for the fullness of God.

GARDEN MOMENTS
for Your Soul

What things have your heart tied up in knots?

....

....

....

....

....

....

....

Do you tend to pour out your heart to God or do you keep things tucked inside?

....

....

....

....

....

....

Consider writing down a list of all the things that are on your heart (nothing is too small or silly). Record each thing that is distracting you, stealing your joy, or concerning you, and begin pouring it all out to God.

....

....

....

....

....

....

Pray

Father, You are my Comforter and my all-knowing and always-present God. Thank You for being my Helper and Deliverer. Thank You for loving me so personally and completely. Lord, here are all the things that have my heart tied up in knots today. (Pour out those things here.) Will You come into these things and help me? Help me pour out my heart daily to make room for Your peace and love. I lay it all before You and ask You to sweep out my anxiety and set my heart right again. Thank You for taking my burdens, no matter how silly, selfish, or little they seem to me. Thank You that through this pouring out of my heart to You, I find You. I grow in my faith. I know You deeper. Thank You for the gift of communicating with You and pouring out my heart to You. Pour Your love and grace into me.

Still Waters

> *Today let your heart settle into God. Let Him undo your stress. Let Him have your anxiety. Be still awhile with the One who loves to still your storms to a whisper.*

He stilled the storm to a whisper;
the waves of the sea were hushed.

PSALM 107:29 NIV

TODAY I WANT TO FOCUS on the theme of stillness that echoes throughout Scripture. Let's dive into some of the places in Scripture where we find an invitation to simply be still and focus on the One who is able to still our storms.

The LORD will fight for you; you need only to be still. (Exod. 14:14 NIV)

Be still before the LORD and wait patiently for him. (Ps. 37:7 NIV)

Be still, and know that I am God. (Ps. 46:10 ESV)

In each of these verses, we see that there is power in stillness. There is power in quieting our hearts and doing nothing more than being still before the Lord. Being still is a posture of the heart. It's sitting. It's listening. It's waiting. It's simply knowing God is there. It's remembering He's faithful, He's God, and He's sovereign. Being still is a break for our busy hearts and souls. Being still before God is the best kind of soul rest.

Clearly, for us busy gals, finding moments of silence and quiet is tricky. Many of us enjoy being in constant motion. I think that's why for me sometimes it feels a lot easier to pray than to take moments to be still. Praying gives me an agenda, something to work through. Being still is more challenging because I easily get lured into motion again by the phone alerting me, the next chore that needs attention, and other things. But let's think of being still in a way that will motivate us to want to take those quiet moments with God. What if we remembered there is power in the stillness, in simply sitting with God? What if we believed He will whisper precious truth to our soul that applies perfectly to our current worry? What if we believed He will remind us of the ways He's been faithful in the past? What if we expected His soothing, calming presence to be the balm our souls desperately need in that particular moment? And what if we integrated these still moments into our day often?

The author of Psalm 107 depicts how God rescued and protected the sailors on their oceanic journey. Let's take a look at what led up to that moment:

> Others went to sea in ships,
> conducting trade on the vast water.
> They saw the LORD's works,
> his wonderful works in the deep.
> He spoke and raised a stormy wind
> that stirred up the waves of the sea.
> Rising up to the sky,
> sinking down to the depths,
> their courage melting away in anguish,
> they reeled and staggered like a drunkard,
> and all their skill was useless.
> Then they cried out to the LORD in their trouble,
> and he brought them out of their distress.
> He stilled their storm to a whisper,
> and the waves of the sea were hushed. (vv. 23–29)

In this situation, God literally hushed the waves and calmed a physical storm. These sailors had lost all courage. They were afraid. I'm sure they were excellent sailors, but they came to a point of realizing that their skills were not enough to save them. So they cried out to God, and He so beautifully calmed everything down and saved their lives. What a gorgeous picture of what God wants to do for us every day in whatever storms we are facing. While our modern-day storms may not involve deep water and treacherous waves, the weight of them can feel just as scary and overwhelming. Our circumstances can grow stormy, and the storm affects our hearts. We run out of solutions and quick fixes. We come to a place where we don't know what else to do. The psalmist reminds us that God can still our storms. Just like the sailors, we can cry out to God and He will bring us out of our distress. Over and over again He calms our storms to a whisper. There are going to be storms: "I have told you these things so that in me you may have peace. You will have suffering in this world. Be courageous! I have conquered the world" (John 16:33). But in every storm, we have the One who has the power to calm it.

Worry depletes. Worry entangles. Worry discourages. Worry suppresses joy. But because of Jesus, we have a quiet place to shake off the worries. We have the One, the God of the universe, who says, "Do not worry about your life" (Matt. 6:25 NIV). He has lived as a human and is fully aware of all there is to worry about, and yet He urges us *not* to worry. Instead, He invites us to "be still, and know that [He is] God" (Ps. 46:10 ESV). He invites us to bring Him our worries every single day and simply rest in knowing He is working them out.

Daughter of Christ, let every worry be an opportunity to invite God in. Let every worry be an invitation to come and be still before Him. Maybe you've already poured out your heart to God in regard to a particular worry and you're simply waiting for Him to work it out. Just know He's God. Know He's at work behind the scenes. Know He's faithful.

Without worries, would we need God in the same way? Without our very human hearts, would we need a Savior? I would love life without worries, but I love life with God more. Worries open the door to opportunities to experience God in a deeper way as He stills our concerns. I wonder what your sweet heart is worried about today. Will you meet

Him in the wings of life where no one sees, in the secrecy of you and God, and simply set down your worries before Him and still your heart? He wants to surround you with His love and assure you of His fixed gaze on you, your life, and your current concerns.

Being still before God gives our hearts a chance to remember and know deep in our bones . . . *yes, He's God.* Being still before God puts the situation or worry in His capable arms and gives Him room to fight our battles for us. Being still before God gives our hearts space to wait on Him, trusting that He's in control. In our quiet moments with God, He stills our inner storms. It's in the quiet that we find reprieve. It's in the still moments that our worries subside into the vast ocean of God's care and provision. He gladly calms our storms as we still our hearts in His presence. Our be-still moments are moments to remember that we are God's beloved daughters and that He is faithful, strong, and capable of taking care of those things we may not know how to pray for or how to handle. Be still, dear daughter, and entrust every worry to the One who longs to care for your heart. He is faithful.

GARDEN MOMENTS
for Your Soul

What worries are weighing heavily on you today?

....

....

....

....

....

How do you typically deal with the worries of your heart?

....

....

....

....

....

How can you practice being still before God?

....

....

....

....

....

· · · · · · · · ·   **Pray**   · · · · · · · · ·

Jesus, I long to live free of worry. I long to live with Your deep peace. I realize I tend to carry my worries for as long as I can. I try to fix the things that are worrying me. I reach for my solutions, my answers. But You, sweet Lord, invite me to be still. You invite me to bring You each worry and let You come into every situation.

Will You help me meet You in the quiet and stillness? Will You change me to desire to bring You every worry so that I can live with Your deep peace, knowing You are at work in my circumstances and my heart? Give me grace to trust You more and to lean on You. Unchain my heart from worry. Make me steady in You as I learn this new dance of being still before You and letting You have my worries. Thank you for choosing to dance through life with me, through every worry.

DAY 12

Be Restored

Let Jesus restore you to your true self. He knows you better than you know yourself, and He loves everything about you. He wants you to be free to be the gal He made you to be. Lean in close. Listen for His gentle whispers of love to your soul. Lean in and be restored.

GOD, your God, will restore everything you
lost; he'll have compassion on you; he'll
come back and pick up the pieces from all
the places where you were scattered.

DEUTERONOMY 30:3 MESSAGE

ONE OF THE SWEETEST PARTS OF RETREATING with the Lord and taking the time to hone in on His heart for you is that you actually begin to find the real, true you. Maybe she got lost somewhere down the line. Maybe she is tucked deeply within you, hunkering down under expectations, suppressed by comparisons, trying so hard to be like anybody but herself. Have you ever felt like you are not sure who you are because you have been trying to be like everyone else? Or maybe you simply feel so busy that you haven't really taken the time to discover who God created you to be. The real you is still in there—and she's beautiful. Jesus wants to restore her and set her free.

Themes of restoration and returning to the Lord are laced throughout the book of Deuteronomy, and I love today's verse in particular. This verse shows us that God is passionate about restoring our hearts. He's a gatherer. He gathers all the parts of us that feel lost, hurt, empty, or unsure and puts us back together in a sense.

God, our sweet and loving Father, actually wants to bring out the real us. He wants to mend the broken, scarred, or wounded places in our hearts. He even wants to mend the places where we feel a bit lost. He wants to show us who He made us to be, because when we let Him restore us to our real selves, we'll flourish. He wants us to flourish. And I think it's rare that we pause and slow down enough to bring God these tender pieces of our hearts and souls and allow Him to rebuild us into what He wants us to be.

Psalm 147:2–3 says, "The LORD rebuilds Jerusalem; he gathers Israel's exiled people. He heals the brokenhearted and bandages their wounds." He loves the real you because He created you. I know you have heard it a million times, but have you let it sink in? You are made by God, and the last thing He wants you to do is suppress who you really are. Instead of suppressing you, He wants to rebuild you, gather you, and heal you. He wants to bring out the real you as you draw close to His heart. As you draw close, He restores you.

I imagine God wants us to be our true selves. How do we do that? It seems like kind of a silly question, but many of us have gotten so deep into striving to be like others or so scattered by our own striving to find ourselves that we're not sure how to be ourselves.

We can start becoming our full selves by admitting we need His restoration. Once we admit we need help putting away our quests to be like that gal over there instead of the gal right here, He intercedes. He helps us check our motivations and notice when we are trying to mimic others instead of being ourselves. Here is some encouraging news too: the only one we need to mimic is Christ. As we look to Him and know Him, we become who we were meant to be. It's a lifelong process to become more like Jesus, and the result is that we find our truest selves.

At some point in my ballet career, after looking around way too much to find out who I was made to be instead of looking to God, I made a conscious choice to be Sarah. It was around the time I had my first baby and saw how perfect and unique he was. I remember thinking I would never want to change a thing about him. His head of dark hair, deep brown eyes, those rosy little lips, and that precious little temperament seemed so perfect. I wonder if that's how God feels about us. I wonder if He looks at us, made perfectly in His image, and hopes we love and appreciate our uniqueness as much as He does. Having my own child helped me see how unique I was too. And I decided to get busy being me. Instead of dressing or dancing like that principal dancer, I embraced my long legs and danced like me. Instead of watching her constantly, I kept my eyes on the Lord, trusting His way in me. That shift in focus helped me find myself again.

God began to restore the real me. And He wants to restore the real you.

You need to know this too: you are beautiful right now. You are beautiful today. Does God want to grow you into a woman after His heart, shape you, and rebuild you? Absolutely. But know that all the growing and blossoming begins by first understanding that you're already lovely. Sometimes we can get so caught up in becoming a better version of ourselves that we miss the beauty we already possess. Yes, you are in-process, but your beginning state is no less beautiful than where God is leading you to. Embrace your beauty. Own it. Be you. Start there. And let God restore the rest.

As you lock eyes with your Maker, you will find the real you again. She's in there, waiting to be set free. The things you see as weaknesses God wants to use. He put them there so you would need Him. Needing Him is the first step to being fully restored. He wants to set your heart free. He wants you to see the treasure of being you. Will you step into this restoring dance with Him? Will you take His hand? Turn your eyes to Him and be restored.

GARDEN MOMENTS
for Your Soul

In what ways have you been trying to be like other gals?

....

....

How does it make you feel when you are in constant improvement mode?

Consider today's verse. How has the Lord been good to you? And how might He want to restore your heart back to being your true self?

• • • • • • • • •   Pray   • • • • • • • •

God, You know me better than I know myself. I am sorry for the ways I have gotten tangled up in trying to be like everybody but myself. Thank You for being a God of restoration. You bring out the real me. Thank You for showing me that the real me is beautiful and that living my life as the real me is the most freeing way to live. I admit that I have weaknesses. There are things I wish I could change. But today You invite me to release my desire to be like others and instead embrace being the gal You made me to be. Will You open my eyes to see who she is? Will You give me a new appreciation for her? Will You begin a restoring work inside me and help me find her again? Lord, help me keep my eyes and heart on You so that I can stay free to be me. When I look around too much, I lose me because my heart tries to mimic others. Help me look to You. Keep my eyes on You. Set me free to be the gal You had in mind when You created me. The ways You work to restore, help, and love me are amazing. Thank You for loving me so personally and so unconditionally. I am ready to dance my dance as myself. Thank You that when I get back to being me, I get to enjoy my dance with You even more.

DAY 13

Soul-Nourishment

Today soak in the beauty of God's Word. Reflect on the tangible gift of His Word, which you get to hold and ponder. Your soul was created to be nourished by God's Word. Discover anew the richness, fullness, abundance, and joy of God's love letter to you.

You're my place of quiet retreat;
I wait for your Word to renew me.

PSALM 119:114 MESSAGE

FOR US TO FUNCTION WELL, our souls need nourishment. Our souls are what I like to think of as the spiritual side of us. It's the place where we feel, where we live from. I don't understand all the intricacies and differences between a person's heart, soul, and mind, but I do know that a girl can tell when her soul's just not right. Luke 10:27 says,

"[Jesus] answered, 'Love the Lord your God with all your heart and with all your soul and with all your strength and with all your mind'" (NIV). Heart. Soul. Strength. Mind. All these elements of our humanity seem to work together to make us who we are, and when one of them is malnourished, something feels off. I love that Jesus commands us to love Him with all the aspects of ourselves, and maybe when we do, all the parts of us fall beautifully into place. One thing I've learned about the Word through the years of my own growing is that it settles, satisfies, and renews my soul. It's the perfect soul-nourishment. The Word makes my soul right again. Maybe part of loving God with all our souls is growing to love His Word.

Today let's talk about the Word and why it's the go-to source for soul-nourishment. Today's verse describes God as "my place of quiet retreat." That statement encompasses what the pages of this book are about, and I pray if we get anything from our thirty days together it's that we see God is our place of quiet retreat. Always. Every day. Every moment. The rest of the verse goes on to say, "I wait for your Word to renew me." As we talked about earlier, spiritual growth and renewal aren't instantaneous. They are a process. And they involve waiting. Sometimes I get in this kind of drive-through mentality about my time with God and His Word. Sometimes in my fast pace, I quickly get in my time with Him and then move on to the rest of my day. His grace whispers to my soul that that's okay, no need to be hard on myself for a quick quiet time. But today's verse opens my eyes to see and remember that renewal through God's Word—this rich soul-nourishment—takes time and space. And to have time and space, I must slow down.

We've talked about some of the challenges in our day and age with creating and keeping this space in our souls for God. It's a real struggle to slow down, to pause, and to be still. Instead of seeing it as a horribly negative thing we face every single day, let's see it as a thrilling challenge to make room for God's renewal. To make room for God to whisper to our hearts, shape us with His Word, and change the way we think and live.

Hebrews 4:12 says, "For the word of God is living and effective and sharper than any double-edged sword, penetrating as far as the separation of soul and spirit, joints and marrow. It is able to judge the ideas and thoughts of the heart" (HCSB). I love that there is heart and soul in this verse. The Word of God digs into every part of us. The Word isn't just a book of historical facts and stories. It's alive with God's Spirit, permeating our hearts with the very breath of God. And His Word in us makes our souls, hearts, and minds right. His Word, as the psalmist says, is "sweeter than honey" (Ps. 119:103 NIV). And we have to make room for the sweetness. It takes time to linger over it and let it soak in. It takes space for it to resonate with us and take hold of our hearts and souls. It takes time for it to marinate in us and change us. It takes slowing down to make room for renewal through God's Word. This doesn't mean we have to read for a certain number of minutes per day or stick to a reading plan perfectly. There's not a formula to follow here, but today let's see the beauty of making space for God's Word to do renewing work in our souls.

Our little crew was at family camp last summer, and I remember one day being caught off guard by one camp counselor's love for her Bible. She was running the Screamer (an incredibly fun but terrifying and high trapeze contraption in which my sons basically swing through the trees with sheer joy, and I squirm on the inside because it's totally scary and awesome all wrapped up in one). Anyways, this sweet gal had a lot of downtime in between each kiddo's turn to ride the Screamer, so she sat on a bench nearby, just her and her Bible. Her Bible was bulky but fit in the crook of her arm perfectly. It was wrapped in a cute patterned cover with highlighters and pens (be still my heart!) peeking out of its little side pocket. I could tell it was one well-loved Bible. Between helping kiddos swing through the trees, she opened the Bible up, and the best way I can describe it is that she glowed from within as she read. I visited with her later and asked her about her cute, patterned Bible cover, and with pure joy and light radiating from within, she told me all about it. It was evident that she loved her Bible—and her Lord. As the kiddos and I moved on to our next activity, I remember thinking, *I want to love my Bible and my Lord like that.*

I'd had a Bible for as long as I could remember, but this precious gal inspired me to see it as the precious gift that it is—to hold it close, dig in, and discover the treasures laced through the pages. Another thing that amazed me about her was that she kept her Bible with her. It was practically a part of her, like a purse would be. It was part of her everyday life, and it was beautifully impacting the state of her soul. I may or may not have gotten myself a cute, patterned Bible cover when we got home, and I may or may not have ordered some fun highlighters. The point for me wasn't about making my Bible more colorful; it was about refreshing my love for God's Word. It was about stirring up excitement for the Word that I knew was within me but had gotten a bit weighed down by my worries and cares. Mark 4:19–20 says, "But the worries of this age, the deceitfulness of wealth, and the desires for other things enter in and choke the word, and it becomes unfruitful. And those like seed sown on good ground hear the word, welcome it, and produce fruit thirty, sixty, and a hundred times what was sown." Maybe the details of life were somewhat choking the Word right out of me and my own busy heart was keeping the Word from being fruitful in that season. I craved to make space to hear the Word in a fresh way, to welcome it as it says in Mark, and to trust that God will produce the fruit I long for in my spiritual life.

Maybe you're in a place where God's Word is fresh, new, and exciting to you. Or maybe you're in a season where the Word feels more like homework than soul-nourishment. Wherever you are, I hope today encourages you to see God's Word in a new light. I hope you see that His Word is where He whispers to you, it's how He lavishes you with His truth and love, and it's how He renews you day by day to do and be all that He's created you to do and be. It's where your relationship with God is cultivated. So whether you're a "Bible cover and highlighters" kind of gal or a "never write in your Bible" kind of gal, you can get excited about God's Word! About the lifetime of treasures He wants to unfold for you as you open your Bible every day. Keep it close, like it's part of you. Run to it when you need nourishment, and keep running to it when you need renewal. God's Word will settle and satisfy your soul. And on top of that, you'll get to know God and know His will as you open His Word. "Do not conform to the pattern of this world, but be transformed by the renewing of your mind. Then you will be able to test and approve what God's will is—his good, pleasing and perfect will" (Rom. 12:2 NIV).

God's Word is how we understand God's ways and how He wants us to live. It's soul-nourishment. It's our guide. It's God's personal whispers to our heart. It's everything.

GARDEN MOMENTS
for Your Soul

Think about a time when God's Word brought you a sense of renewal.

....

....

....

....

....

In this particular season, what role does God's Word play in your life?

....

....

....

....

....

What excites you about stirring up your love for God's Word? What are some practical ways you can grow your affection for His Word?

....

....

....

....

....

....

....

. . . . *Pray* . . . .

Lord, thank You for the gift of Your beautiful Word. Thank You that we have access to it daily, and thank You that I get to hear Your whispers over my life through its pages. Lord, increase my delight and love for Your Word. Help me know the sweetness and richness of it. Give me a fresh joy for digging into it, savoring verses, and discovering new things. Open my eyes that I may see wonderful things. Help me make space to linger over and think on Your Word. Let it marinate in my soul and take root in my heart. Thank You that You and Your beautiful Word are my quiet retreat, my constant source of renewal, and my soul's deepest nourishment.

DAY 14

Weed Out the Doubts

> *As you settle into a rhythm with God, notice when weeds of doubt try to creep in. What doubts are disrupting your peace? Making you unsure of God's plans for you? Causing you to fret? Today begins some weed pulling. Weeds of doubt crowd your heart and disrupt your peace. The One who came to bring peace to your soul invites you to be surefooted . . . surehearted.*

And he said to them, "Why are you troubled,
and why do doubts arise in your hearts?"

LUKE 24:38 ESV

Back on day 8, "Prune," we talked about different things, or weeds, that can crowd our hearts. Today I want to talk specifically about one particular pesky weed that can really disrupt our peace and our steady pace with God. This weed is doubt. Doubt is sneaky because it can be subtle. It can manifest itself in many different ways—doubt about God, doubt that He's going to answer our prayers in a specific way, doubt about who He's called us to be and where He's leading us. Keeping the doubts away can feel like a battle, so today I want you to know that it's worth it to keep pulling the weeds of doubt out of the garden of your heart.

We have an enemy who does not want us to walk in God's purposes for us. He does not want us to live with joy, passion, love, and the light of Jesus. He does not want us to be gals who follow after God with all our hearts, minds, and souls. He does not want us to blossom and flourish as God's daughters. And He certainly does not want us to draw closer to God. So he pulls out every trick in the book to deceive, distract, steal joy, and cause us to wilt in doubt. Most times his tactics are subtle. So we must remember that he's lurking (see 1 Pet. 5:8). While we don't need to dwell on the enemy's activity in our lives, we need to be aware of his schemes, otherwise we run the risk of sinking into doubt and missing out on God's peace. So let's think of life as a dance with God but also as a battle against the enemy. Let's remember we have the sword of the Spirit, God's Word, and ultimately God Himself on our side at all times (see Eph. 6:17). Life can be full of dancing and feel less like a battle because the One who has overcome our enemy is with us and working for us at all times. Practically speaking, how do we weed out the doubts that the enemy loves to plant in our hearts?

I wish I had a mapped-out formula for us—a step-by-step dance, if you will, with each move perfectly laid out. But instead, all I know is this: We serve the God of grace. And His battle plan for us is one of trust, faith, the Word, prayer, and surrender. He wants to fight our battles for us. "The LORD will fight for you; you need only to be still" (Exod. 14:14 NIV). His battle plan for us is that we would keep dancing in step with His Spirit, trusting Him day by day, step by step, moment by moment. His battle plan is that we would invite Him to help us stay focused on Him, walk in His purposes for us, preserve joy in us that He has so graciously given us, and help us recognize when doubt is taking over our hearts. So, dancing daughter, don't fret over this enemy who surrounds us. Don't fret about the spiritual battle going on in and around us at all times. Know that the One who created you fights for you. Know that He's already won the battle for your salvation and for this world. Keep your ears perked for the quiet whisper of God in your days. Tune your heart to His grace and know the power of God inside you as you trust Him moment by moment. Pray that the enemy will steer clear of you because you are a daughter in tune with her Savior. Refocus when you feel like you've gotten caught up in the enemy's schemes.

Specifically talk to the Lord about the areas in your life in which you feel a sense of doubt. What are you doubting about God Himself? What are you doubting about His faithfulness? What are you doubting about His plans for you or for the world we live in?

Doubt is an opportunity to let God speak into our hearts and remind us of who He is, His faithful character, and His promises. God wants to help us pull the weeds of doubt that are keeping our hearts from fully flourishing.

Weeds in a garden are pesky. The weeds in my own backyard can be quite stubborn. They grow fast too. They are determined little things, trying hard to overtake and outdo the beautiful plants and flowers I want to grow. It's a continual job to keep the weeds under control.

So it is with our hearts. Doubt is pesky, stubborn, and determined. And so is our enemy. He works overtime to get our doubts to overtake and outdo the beauty God produces in our hearts, the fruit of the Spirit—love, joy, peace, patience, kindness, goodness, faithfulness, gentleness, and self-control (see Gal. 5:22–23).

Jesus asked the disciples, "Why are you troubled, and why do doubts arise in your hearts?" (Luke 24:38 ESV). He must know that something in our human nature is hardwired toward doubt. Maybe sometimes the enemy is taunting us and feeding our doubts, or maybe sometimes our own feelings of unbelief cause doubt in our hearts. Wherever the doubt is coming from, Jesus does not want us to be troubled. He wants us to live in peace. "Peace to you!" (Luke 24:36 ESV).

Today's verse comes from a section in Luke in which Jesus revealed Himself to His disciples after He had risen from the grave. He went on to say,

> "Look at my hands and my feet, that it is I myself! Touch me and see, because a ghost does not have flesh and bones as you can see I have." Having said this, he showed them his hands and feet. But while they still were amazed and in disbelief because of their joy, he asked them, "Do you have anything here to eat?" (vv. 39–41)

Jesus convinced the disciples of His reality. He wanted them to know it was really Him. He was standing right there in their presence. And I love how Jesus moved on with the moment so casually by asking if they had anything to eat. His need for food made the reality of Himself even more tangible and convincing.

What if the answer to our weeds of doubt, which we so desperately would like pulled from the garden of our hearts, is to focus on the reality of Jesus? The more we focus on His reality, the less we will feel doubts creep into our own everyday realities. When we remember that it's Him—He's real, He's right here in the middle of the everyday moments—our weeds of doubt lose their hold on our hearts.

Life is a dance and a battle. Doubt is going to try to creep into our hearts and make us question God and His ways. But we always have the reality of Jesus in our day. And as we focus on Him and hand over our doubts to Him, we can live with His peace. It's an over and over again cycle of pulling these pesky weeds of doubt, but it keeps us dependent on Him. Every time we have a thought that leans toward doubt, we can catch it and give it over to the One who offers peace. Remember 2 Corinthians 10:5: "We demolish arguments and every pretension that sets itself up against the knowledge of God, and we take captive every thought to make it obedient to Christ" (NIV).

Whatever doubts are taking hold of your heart and for however long they have been weighing it down, know today that Jesus does not want you to live in doubt. He wants to pull those doubts out and away from your heart and set you free to know His peace, His reality, and His truth. Set every doubt before Him, and let Him speak truth into your heart. Let Him make over the garden of your heart with His peace.

GARDEN MOMENTS
for Your Soul

What doubts have been crowding your heart? Doubts about God? Doubts about His plans for you? Doubts about His goodness?

....

....

....

....

....

....

How can you take these thoughts captive today and allow God to minister His peace to you?

....

....

....

....

....

....

· · · · · · · · · · **Pray** · · · · · · · · · ·

*Jesus, thank You for coming to set us free. Thank You
for inviting us into the abundant life of truth, grace,
and peace. Lord, You know exactly what doubts are
crowding my heart. I lay each of them before You today
and ask You to weed them out and replace them with
Your deep peace. And every time I feel those weeds of
doubt creeping back into my heart, help me notice.
Remind me to bring them to You so You can shed Your
light on them and help me see Your truth. Thank You
for always being in my midst, working in and around
me. Here is every weed of doubt. Speak truth into my
heart today and set my heart free to flourish in peace.*

DAY 15

Grow Grateful

Linger in gratefulness today. As we grow grateful, our hearts open up to God's goodness. Reflecting on His goodness builds our faith and teaches us to enjoy life at God's pace. Our delight for God increases. Then we ourselves exude gratefulness, putting the spotlight on the Giver of every good and perfect gift. What are you grateful for?

Every good and perfect gift is from above, coming down from the Father of the heavenly lights, who does not change like shifting shadows.

JAMES 1:17 NIV

BACK IN OUR READING ON CULTIVATING, we talked through what it looks like to cultivate contentment. Today I want to take it a step further and talk specifically about gratefulness and why growing grateful is important to our everyday life. I know "growing in gratefulness" can feel like a parental pep talk that makes us squirm a bit. We realize we should be grateful. So let's discover the beauty in gratefulness, knowing God can expand our hearts to ultimately experience even more abundant life in Him.

In the book of James, we are challenged to see good in the trials of life. James 1:2–4 says, "Consider it a great joy, my brothers and sisters, whenever you experience various trials, because you know that the testing of your faith produces endurance. And let endurance have its full effect, so that you may be mature and complete, lacking nothing." My first response to most trials is certainly not joy or gratefulness. I go straight to dread, fear, worry, or stress. But here James shows us that the trials of life test our faith and produce endurance. This life, while brief in the grand scheme of eternity, is full of testing and trials. It's not always easy. We have a long way to go on our journeys. So we need endurance to keep going. Fatigue, stress, and other adverse conditions along our path require strength to get us through them. As James states, when endurance takes its full effect in us, we become complete and mature—lacking nothing.

Developing endurance begins with a choice to *consider* ("to think carefully about, especially in order to make a decision; contemplate; reflect on").[1] We must choose to see trials from a new perspective. We must choose gratefulness. And when we do, our faith gains traction and we are strengthened for the next leg of our journey.

Think of someone in your life who exudes this kind of attitude. We all probably have people in our lives who glow with a grateful heart. They rarely, if ever, complain. They seem to see the bright side of every situation. And you can tell their hearts are happy, content, and at peace. These kinds of folks draw us in and make us want to be around them. Their own joy and gratefulness are contagious. We also know people who carry a negative vibe with them wherever they go. They seem mad at everything. They pick out the problem in every situation. And they aren't super fun to be around. Sometimes we are that person (raising my own hand here). I long to be like the people who exude a sense of gratitude in all they do. Some people may be more naturally grateful than others, but we can all grow grateful with God's help. Growing grateful will affect not only our own hearts but also the hearts of those around us.

Gratefulness flips the switch, turning a negative situation into an opportunity to lean on the Lord and watch Him work. Gratefulness helps us have an "I get to do this" attitude instead of an "I have to." Everything from the small, mundane tasks of the day to the big, exciting life moments becomes an opportunity to see God at work. Gratefulness stirs up our passion, reminds us that God is with us, and gives us the endurance to keep going when things are rocky.

If I were to look out at my backyard and simply focus on the mess (the weeds that need pulling, the grass that needs mowing, the toys that need picking up, the fence that needs repairing), I would miss the beauty. But if I flip the switch, in a sense, and focus on the good stuff (that one rose that bloomed, the plants beginning to come back after winter, the kiddos who enjoy the backyard, the signs of spring that are becoming noticeable), my perspective changes completely. It gives me energy to keep doing the hard work of maintaining the garden, it gives me joy to simply savor the beauty, and it gives me a sense of peace knowing that while there is always a mess of some sort, the mess is being made into something beautiful.

Maybe lately you've only been able to consider the mess in your life. You see the stuff that needs to be weeded out, you spot what needs improvement, and you wish this or that could be different. But what if you dug for the beauty? What if you intentionally looked for things to be grateful for in your life, in your relationship with the Lord, and in the beauty of what God has placed before you in this season? How might your change of perspective affect everything?

When we dig in and grow gratefulness right there in the messy trials of life, our faith is strengthened, our spiritual roots grow deeper, and our love for God becomes sweeter. We begin to see that each trial draws us closer to our Master Gardener if we let it. And as we grow grateful and consider each trial with joy, we are energized.

As we turn our focus to Him, and all that we have in Him, gratefulness becomes a natural outpouring of our hearts. Gratefulness, this choice to consider trials joy and to express thanks to God, opens the door to worship. Take a look at Psalm 100:

> Let the whole earth shout triumphantly to God!
> Serve the LORD with gladness;
> come before him with joyful songs.
> Acknowledge that the LORD is God.
> He made us, and we are his—
> his people, the sheep of his pasture.
> Enter his gates with thanksgiving
> and his courts with praise.
> Give thanks to him and bless his name.

For the LORD is good, and his faithful love endures
  forever;
his faithfulness, through all generations.

As we grow grateful to God for all that we have in Him,
it spills out into everything we do. As we worship God, we
find the faith and endurance to keep going. Worship flips our
perspective. Worship opens the pathway to a deeper sense of
God's presence. Worship changes everything.

So begin today to see the beauty in growing grateful.
Express your thanks to God throughout your day by whispering prayers of gratitude. Thank Him for everything from
His big gift of salvation to the little gift of something tangible in your day that blessed you. Thank Him for the people
He's put in your life, the ways He's faithfully guided you,
and His constant presence in your life. Choose gratefulness
and experience a deepening of your faith. And be honest
with God when gratefulness is hard. Express the whys and
frustrations to Him. Talk it out with Him. By His grace
and with His Spirit, He will gladly help you grow grateful. "But the Helper, the Holy Spirit, whom the Father will
send in my name, he will teach you all things and bring to
your remembrance all that I have said to you" (John 14:26
ESV).

Remember today that growing grateful changes everything. Growing grateful is deepening your faith, blessing others with the lightness of a thankful heart, and spotlighting
the One from whom all good gifts come. Let gratefulness
stir up your joy and open your heart to more of God. Let
the work of growing grateful give you the endurance to keep
going and dancing in God's purposes for you.

GARDEN MOMENTS
for Your Soul

How have choosing joy and growing grateful been hard for you in this season?

....

....

....

....

What excites you about growing grateful?

....

....

....

....

What specific things are you grateful for in your relationship with God?

....

....

....

....

....

· · · · · · · · · · **Pray** · · · · · · · · ·

Lord, thank You for a moment to focus on the gift of gratitude and the way it can flip the switch in my faith and attitude. Thank You for being who You are, for all that You have done for me, and for how You continuously draw me closer to You. Thank You that I can honor you by focusing on You and making a sacrifice of thanksgiving to You. Lord, I want to honor You. I want to be the type of gal who exudes joy, draws others to you, and is a blessing to be around. I long to be deeply rooted in peace and joy, and I need Your Spirit to grab my attention when I'm overly focused on the negative parts of a trial. Help me see You in every trial. Help me embrace the gift of being Your daughter. Thank You for always being there for me. May my life be an offering of praise, thanksgiving, and gratitude as I walk through trials with You.

Love Lavishly

> *As you slow your pace, savor God's Word, and draw closer to God, your soul will be fed. And when your soul is fed with God's love, the overflow will pour out onto others. Today focus on the gift of loving God, loving others, and loving yourself well from a place of being loved lavishly by the One who created you. God gives you the power to love well, and it begins with knowing how deeply He loves you.*

We love because he first loved us.

———

1 JOHN 4:19 ESV

ONE OF THE FRUITS THAT GROWS out of our time with God is the fruit of love. According to Galatians 5:22, "The fruit of the Spirit is love" (NIV). Love is clearly important to God, and it's something the Spirit works in us as we draw close to Him. Themes of love are sprinkled throughout Scripture and point us to God, who lavishes His love on us and wants us to love others and ourselves out of this divine love. One reason I crave quiet retreats with God is so that I can be filled up in order to love well. The people in my life certainly love me well, and I desperately want to love them well back. But when a gal is on empty, as I'm sure you've experienced, it's hard to love well. Today let's rehearse truth to our hearts about how loving well requires that we be loved well. Let's remind ourselves of how God has lavished His love on us and how we can love like Jesus loves.

I think our automatic assumption when we talk about loving well is loving others. And, absolutely, that is one piece of the pie of loving well. Jesus said, "You shall love the Lord your God with all your heart and with all your soul and with all your mind. This is the great and first commandment. And a second is like it: You shall love your neighbor as yourself" (Matt. 22:37–39 ESV). As women, we work hard at loving well. We find ways to serve, we sign up to help, we work to meet the needs of others, and we do our best to do it all well. But too often we wear ourselves out trying so hard to love well and serve well that we miss that Jesus never said not to love and care for ourselves. He doesn't ask us to wear ourselves thin and forget about our own needs. But He does call us to look to the interests of others (see Phil. 2:4) and to love others as well as we care and tend our own lives and hearts. I think many of us, in our efforts to love well, can easily let our care for our own hearts, minds, and bodies go. And we wind up quite depleted.

Let's take a look at Jesus's example of how He lived and loved. Of course, Jesus loved in the ultimate way by dying on the cross for humankind; but in His everyday life, He loved in simple ways. He urges us to do the same throughout the

Bible. "He has told you, O man, what is good; and what does the LORD require of you but to do justice, and to love kindness, and to walk humbly with your God?" (Mic. 6:8 ESV). He speaks of simple acts of kindness, such as giving water to someone who is thirsty (see Matt. 10:42), loving the poor, orphaned, and widowed (see Isa. 1:17), and going the extra mile (see Matt. 5:41). He calls us to a daily pattern of loving as we walk with Him. As He puts people in our path, He asks us to choose kindness, care, and love.

As women, we tend to want to do a major project of love or sign up for something big and missional in order to love well. And those are beautiful things if we have the capacity to take them on in our current season. But what I want us to see today is that our everyday lives present opportunities to love well. This can be true in the simplest things—sending an email with a kind tone, making a phone call to a friend, checking in with our spouse to encourage them in their day, opening the door for a stranger and saying hello with a smile, putting down the phone and listening well to the person in front of us, doing that chore that feels unseen but you know will bless your family. It's the little things. So whether we are taking on some big act of service or love that we have capacity for or we are growing little by little in our efforts to really see and care for the people right in front of us, remember that our desire and ability to love in these ways comes from God. "We love because he first loved us" (1 John 4:19 NIV). And He gives us all we need to love well. While we do have to choose to love in the moment, because of course it doesn't come naturally to us, God is making over our nature as we lean on Him. And He gives us the power and desire to love as we draw near to Him. So loving well flows out of our relationship with God. As we focus on how much He loves us in our imperfect state and consider His commandment that we love others, our desire and passion to love in the everyday things increase. And He will be faithful to help us love well.

Daughter of Christ, when you love others and love that gal God made you to be—quirks and all—you're loving God. You don't have to do more for God or prove your love to Him. As you walk day to day with Him and open your heart to little ways He's asking you to love others and yourself, you're loving God. You're worshiping the One who loves you dearly. Take a look at John 13:34–35:

> I give you a new command: Love one another. Just as I have loved you, you are also to love one another. By this everyone will know that you are my disciples, if you love one another.

The way we love one another and those around us draws people to God. Our love for another points to the gospel. The way we love should look different, not because we're trying hard but because God's grace and Spirit are flowing through us. Jesus's love in us is how God spreads the gospel.

Many of us may wish we had a laid-out, step-by-step instruction manual for how to love lavishly. And maybe it feels more complicated than it's meant to be. Think of a friend or a parent or a spouse who makes you feel loved. What is it in them that makes you feel at ease in their company, loved no matter what, and free to completely be yourself? Think about how you leave their company refreshed. That's what we are aiming for—to love others so that they feel at ease in our company, loved no matter what, and free to completely be themselves. It's a supernatural love that flows from God's heart into ours and out onto another. It can't be explained or mapped out perfectly. Loving others well requires faith and admitting that we can't love well in our own strength. That's a beautiful place for us to start loving lavishly.

I encourage you to talk to the One who loves you dearly and best about how you can operate in His grace pattern of loving well in the day-to-day moments. Express your desire to Him to want to love better. He knows that we get busy and sometimes don't intentionally love well. And that's okay. We are human, gals. But God wants us to experience the joy of loving well. He wants the very best for our relationships. And He wants to continuously draw others to Himself through our gift of love.

So when loving others feels hard, tell Him. Ask for His supernatural grace and help. When it feels impossible or outside your comfort zone, ask Him to help you trust Him. When it feels meaningless or not appreciated, express that to Him. Let Him pour purpose into your heart, helping you see that every act of love—no matter how big or small—is important. And when you feel like you don't have the capacity or energy or time to take on one more thing, talk to Him about it. Ask Him to help you see that it's not about signing up for more things but about loving right where you already are.

Who are the people in your life right now who you can, with God's divine assistance, love well? Who can you surprise with lavish love? Don't underestimate the power of small acts of love: starting up a conversation with that gal you see every day at school pickup, waving to the elderly lady you pass by on your walk, surprising the cashier with a nice comment, picking up the phone to encourage a friend, writing a note to thank someone, giving your spouse your full attention when they are catching you up with their day, getting down on the floor with your kiddos and playing with them—on and on the list goes. It's the little things. Loving well is making a point to notice the opportunities God puts in front of us—not because we're trying to impress or meet some kind of expectation but because God loves us perfectly.

I hope today you see the beauty in loving God and others, appreciating who God made you to be, and embracing God's precious love for you. Let love be your mission. Let the fruit of love blossom in all its fullness as you lean on the One who loves through you.

GARDEN MOMENTS
for Your Soul

What's hard about loving lavishly?

....

....

....

....

....

....

In what ways do you want to love more intentionally, and who in your life do you desire to love lavishly?

....

....

....

....

....

....

....

....

· · · · · · · · · · **Pray** · · · · · · · · ·

God, You are the ultimate description of perfect love. Thank You for loving me by paying my debt on the cross, for loving me enough to open the door to relationship with You. Help me see Your love in a fresh way. Cultivate in me a deeper love for You, for others, and even for myself. Help me love from the well of Your love. Show me little day-to-day moments when I can love others with Your help and grace. Help me choose to love when it feels hard, impossible, or pointless. Help me make others feel loved, at ease, and cared for. Help me see the beauty of loving lavishly, and may it spotlight You. And help me love myself. Help me appreciate the gal You made me to be and treat her with gentleness, kindness, and care. Thank You for loving me lavishly, and give me grace and power to love well.

DAY 17

Like the Birds

Know today that God intends for you to live life without worries consuming your heart. He doesn't want you to live in deep stress, burdened by cares and concerns. He wants you to consider the birds. Watch how they live. Know today that if He cares for the birds, providing all they need, He cares even more for you. He is tenderly nurturing you with all you need.

Therefore I tell you: Don't worry about your life, what you will eat or what you will drink; or about your body, what you will wear. Isn't life more than food and the body more than clothing? Consider the birds of the sky: They don't sow or reap or gather into barns, yet your heavenly Father feeds them. Aren't you worth more than they? Can any of you add one moment to his life-span by worrying?

MATTHEW 6:25–27

We have touched on how worries in particular can crowd our hearts. Today I want to dive a little bit deeper into Jesus's call to not worry. This is difficult. Trying hard to not worry often has the opposite effect on us—we worry more! I don't doubt that you are currently carrying your own plate of worries. I know some of us have serious, maybe even life-threatening situations that make us worry. Whether we are worrying about our schedule, our kiddos, what's for dinner, our future, or a loved one's health, worry is real, and we have plenty to worry about. Yet Jesus gives us this radical instruction to not worry. I think if we had been there in person listening to Him talk about this, we would have raised our hands for more explanation and gotten out our notepads, ready to take notes. We are willing to not worry, but how do we do so when the world we live in and the realities we face every day give us much to fret about?

I love how Jesus points to the simplest things to teach us the hardest lessons. Here in Matthew, He points to the birds of the sky to teach us the life-giving lesson that we don't have to worry about our lives.

When my family and I moved into our home a couple of years ago, one of the first things I could hardly wait to do was to hang baskets of flowers on our front porch. So the second there were hints of spring, I ran to the garden store and purchased beautiful hanging baskets of flowers. I hung them, and let's just say that they ministered to my soul. (It's the little things, right?)

One day a few weeks later, while I stood on a ladder to water my beloved baskets, I leaned in closely to carefully pour in the water and saw two large eyes staring back at me. Thankfully, I did not break anything as I screamed and tumbled off the ladder. The eyes belonged to a mama dove who had made a nest and laid eggs in the hanging basket. We watched every day for the eggs to hatch. Once the eggs hatched, my mama bear instincts kicked in and I found myself worrying about those baby birds. I worried when a storm came through and the hanging baskets swayed from right to left in the wind. I worried the babies would fall out of their nest and be snatched up by our cat. I worried their mama wouldn't come back after leaving to get them food. I worried. Well, one afternoon we had a baby dove incident. The wire holding the basket broke and the babies tumbled out of the nest and onto the ground. Totally freaking out, I convinced my sweet little six-year-old son to put on garden gloves and pick them up tenderly and place them back into their nest. He handled this mission beautifully, and together we got them all back into the nest and hung the basket back up. I breathed a sigh of relief. Later they began learning to fly, and I worried about them when they sat looking quite lost on the front patio as they tried to mimic their flying mama. But all that to say, it fascinated me to see how God took care of this little dove family. I had to trust that they knew what they were doing.

As I think about Jesus saying "consider the birds," it excites me to know He wants us to realize that He knows what He's doing with us. We hover over our situations, worrying and trying to handle things, and we even try to help God along in a way. But when we step back and allow Him to do what He does—to tenderly care for each concern and work out things in the way He sees fit—we discover that He's in control. He's good. And He's so good at doing what He does—being God.

God wants us to step out of the way and let Him handle our worries. He talks about how the birds don't sow or reap or gather in barns. They aren't planning out their lives and scrambling to make sure they have enough of what they need from day to day. Now, I don't think that means we don't have to plan or save up or be smart about our lives. Instead, it's an invitation to lean on God's sufficiency and grace. And to trust that He's going to give us just what we need for this day, which will add up to a string of days throughout our lifetime.

This makes me think of manna. The Israelites were starving and wondered how they would survive. But God had an answer: "Then the LORD said to Moses, 'I am going to rain bread from heaven for you. The people are to go out each day and gather enough for that day'" (Exod. 16:4). God faithfully rained down this heaven-sent bread to His people but instructed them to gather only what they needed for that day. That way the manna was always fresh. God provided just the right amount of sustenance for each day. In the same way, we can trust God each day to provide us with all we need to be who He's calling us to be and to walk in His purposes. He will provide everything we need through the manna of His Word, the gift of His Spirit, and His life-giving presence. And like the birds, we can be busy being who God has called us to be and doing what God has called us to do—to be loved and to love well. And we can entrust the rest—our worries—to Him.

God went to the trouble of making our earth beautiful, sprinkling it with birds and flowers and mountains and oceans. He didn't have to do that. But as we look on creation, we see that it ministers back to us and points us to Him. It's beautiful how the birds gather just what they need day to day. Today is an invitation to learn from the birds. God cared enough about these sweet little creatures to dream up so many different kinds and types and colors. If He cares so much about the birds, how much more does He care about you and your life?

Worrying is hard to let go of, but living free of worry is something Jesus wants for us. So it must be possible. May we be inspired to bring every worry to God the second we feel it take its hold on us. May we give God every worry and trust Him to work it out for His glory. May we see our tendency to worry as an opportunity to lean into God and converse with Him.

The deeper we get to know God, the more space we make for Him to fill up our hearts and the more we will default to trusting Him instead of worrying. It's another dance. It's a dance we learn day to day. And oftentimes we stumble. We get caught up in the worries of life and find ourselves stressed-out and anxious. Then He whispers quietly to our hearts that He can be trusted. So we get back up on our feet, take His hand, and begin again this dance of trusting our Maker. We trust that He made us and that He cares for us. We trust that He's guiding every step and providing for our every need along the way. We trust that He's got our future, our loved ones, and our everything in between. So we dance on, and we taste the joy and freedom of life with Him, entrusting our worries to Him. Then another worry begins to gnaw at us. But this time, instead of completely losing our balance and falling into a heap, we remember this: *He's trustworthy. He's God. He's in control.* And this time we bring our worries to Him. We tell Him the things that have our hearts tied up in knots. And we let Him do what He does best—sort us out, calm the storm inside us to a whisper, and tell us that all is well.

All that concerns us is in God's hands. And so we keep dancing with Him through all of life. We won't dance it perfectly. We will stumble into worry mode more often than we like. But as we experience the divine peace that comes when we release our worries to our Maker and trust Him day by day, we grow more and more dependent on Him. And a gal dependent on her Maker lives like the birds—she flies, she enjoys the beauty around her, she does her thing, and she trusts that she's tenderly cared for by the God of the universe.

GARDEN MOMENTS
for Your Soul

What worries are you ready to fully turn over to God?

....

....

....

....

Is there a practical way you can remind yourself to consider the birds and trust God when you feel worries crowding your heart?

....

....

· · · · · · · · · · **Pray** · · · · · · · · · ·

Lord, thank You for Your invitation to release my worries to You and trust You with everything. Thank You for the example of the birds and for tenderly caring for them and for me. Help me catch myself when I am letting worries take over my heart and instead turn them over to You through prayer. Build my trust in You as the God of the universe, the One who holds all things together—my cares, my future, my dreams, and everything in between. You hold me together. Remind me that I can trust You with everything. Help me consider the birds, knowing You will provide me with all I need one day at a time.

Like the Wildflowers

You can trust God to provide all you need. You can trust Him with the dreams of your heart and your future. "We know that all things work together for the good of those who love God, who are called according to his purpose" (Rom. 8:28). Daughter of Christ, you can trust God with the everyday, practical necessities of life. He's your Provider. He's your Shepherd. He will guide you, lead you, and care for you.

And why do you worry about clothes? Observe how the wildflowers of the field grow: They don't labor or spin thread. Yet I tell you that not even Solomon in all his splendor was adorned like one of these. If that's how God clothes the grass of the field, which is here today and thrown into the furnace tomorrow, won't he do much more for you—you of little faith? So don't worry, saying, "What will we eat?" or "What will we drink?" or "What will we wear?" For the Gentiles eagerly seek all these things, and your heavenly Father knows

that you need them. But seek first the kingdom of
God and his righteousness, and all these things will
be provided for you. Therefore don't worry about
tomorrow, because tomorrow will worry about
itself. Each day has enough trouble of its own.

MATTHEW 6:28–34

TODAY I WANT TO EXPAND A BIT MORE on this topic
of worry and discuss the small worries of life that often
cause us just as much angst as the big ones. Jesus wants
to show us that He will guide, lead, care, and shepherd us
even in the minor details of life. Even these small worries
can cause havoc and unrest in our hearts, leading us down
a path of stress and anxiety.

Everyday, practical worries are unavoidable. We get a text
message saying one kiddo needs to be here while another
needs to be there, which means we must figure out a way to
be in two places at once. We receive an invitation to something but must work out a conflict in our schedule so we
can attend. A particular thing needs to be done by a certain
day, but it feels like there is no time to pull it all together. We
must remember to turn that paperwork in on this day. We
stress over finding just the right outfit for an event because
we want to look and feel our best (all the gals' hands go up),
but suddenly we don't have *anything* to wear! Or we stress
about our hair or makeup because it's just not quite right. Or
we worry about what to cook when we have company over.
We stress about others' opinions maybe a little more than we
should. Or we worry about our kiddos—sleep, potty training, eating well, getting enough exercise. These thoughts can
consume us if we're not careful.

Obviously, these aren't deep, overwhelming worries, but nevertheless, they cause stress. And the more they pile on top of one another, the more stressed we feel. These everyday worries become roadblocks to our peace. They feed our stress. But the best news is that Jesus does not want us to worry about these things. In the same way that He wants to carry our deeper worries, He also wants to carry our everyday, practical worries. First Peter 5:7 says, "Cast all your anxiety on him because he cares for you" (NIV). All of it. Not just some of it. Not just the big stuff. The little stuff too. And everything in between. I love this little gem in Genesis 18:14: "Is anything too hard for the LORD?" (NIV).

None of your everyday stresses and worries are too hard for the Lord. But gals, I think a lot of us (raising my hand here) forget or don't fully realize that we can bring anything to the Lord. No detail is too small or insignificant for Him. That project you're stressed about, that decision you're working through, that child you're concerned about, that outfit you want to come together for the big event, that money you should save, that sleep you desperately need . . . nothing is too small.

Once again, in Matthew 6:28–34, Jesus points to creation to teach us a lesson about worry. He directs our attention to the wildflowers. In many translations, *lilies* is the term used here, so when I ran across the Christian Standard Bible translation, I may or may not have done a little dance in my kitchen! Jesus invites us to watch how the wildflowers grow. They don't labor and spin. Yet they are so beautiful.

We have a meadow near our house that bursts out in wildflowers in the summer months. It amazes me every year to see the meadow transform from the dry, brown grass of winter to wildflowers of all colors—orange, pink, yellow, white, and purple. The flowers paint the meadow with their bright and happy colors without the help of a gardener. They rely on the sun, the seasons, and the rain to continue in their cycle of beauty.

Jesus points to the way of the wildflowers. He wants us to trust Him to grow us into all He created us to be and to help us live fruitful lives. He wants us to live lives of beauty. But He wants to do the growing, the transforming, and the blossoming. He wants us to trust Him, to rely on Him for all that we need every day. He will keep us in this continual cycle of beauty and growth as we look to Him even in the practical necessities of life. Jesus points out that not even Solomon, a man of wealth and royalty, was dressed as lovely as the wildflowers, and if that's how God clothes the wildflowers, how much more will He clothe you and me? How much more will He provide all that we need to live fruitful lives? He shows us that trusting God with the practical things of life is a faith issue. The practical worries of life are part of our faith. And He wants us to get to a place of entrusting Him with them, just as we entrust Him with the bigger things. Jesus reminds us that the Father knows we need these things. And then Jesus explains the key to trusting God with all the big and small details of life: "Seek first the kingdom of God and his righteousness, and all these things will be provided for you. Therefore don't worry about tomorrow" (Matt. 6:33–34). This is an invitation to let the Lord be lord over every area of our lives—from the big stuff to the small stuff. It's an opportunity to invite God into every detail of our lives. It's a chance to "pray about everything" (Phil. 4:6 NLT) and deepen our relationship with Jesus as we trust Him.

Jesus wants to be your Shepherd through life. "I am the good shepherd. The good shepherd lays down his life for the sheep" (John 10:11 NIV). A shepherd knows the sheep's habits, tendencies, and ways. He's familiar with them. In the same way, Jesus knows us (see Ps. 139:1–6). He knows our habits, our tendencies, and our ways. He's familiar with us because He created us. He knows what we tend to worry about. He knows how our everyday worries tangle our hearts, minds, and souls. And He wants to free us. He wants to take the load of our everyday worries off our backs and carry it for us. No matter how insignificant our current stressor feels, no matter how silly it seems to bring that thing to Him, no matter how minute in the grand scheme of things it may be, it's important to God because it's important to us. He doesn't want us to worry. He invites us to bring it to Him and to allow Him to guide us in this small detail of life too.

Jesus tells us not to worry about tomorrow. As we learn to stay present with God in this very moment today, we are leaving the future—tomorrow and all that entails—to Him. And our hearts thrive like the wildflowers.

GARDEN MOMENTS
for Your Soul

Do you typically give God your everyday worries or do you try to handle them on your own?

....

....

....

....

....

What everyday worries are causing stress in your heart?

....

....

....

....

....

· · · · · · · · · · **Pray** · · · · · · · · ·

Lord, thank You for Your invitation to hand over my everyday stresses and concerns to You. Thank You that nothing is too small or insignificant for You. Here are all the everyday worries that are crowding my heart (list those things here). Help me to daily turn over every care to You and to live fully in the present moment with You. Thank You that You have my tomorrows. Thank You for tending my heart so personally with Your love and care. Thank You for shepherding me and providing all that I need every day.

145

Porch Moments

Today let God whisper to your heart through His creation. Let the sunlight cast rays of joy in your heart. Allow the sounds of nature to minister to your soul. Breathe in the fresh air of a new day. Take in the beauty of His creation.

How countless are your works, LORD!

PSALM 104:24

G OD USES THE BEAUTY of His creation to minister to our hearts and souls. He paints a new sunset in the sky every evening, amazes us with the sheer size of the mountains and vast oceans, and hints of His presence through the beauty of flowers, birds, and spring rain showers. His creation whispers echoes of heaven into our souls. His creation speaks of something other-worldly, something heavenly. His creation declares hope and new life. Today I want to inspire us to soak in the beauty of creation.

My favorite place to soak in God's creation every day is on my back porch. My husband installed a swing on one end of the porch to give us a spot to take in the view. There's nothing fancy about this view. Pots of flowers sit next to the swing; a simple, dusty white table is the perfect spot for a cup of coffee; and the everyday scene includes grass, trees, roses, birds, and our pup. And sprinkled in the midst of it all are bicycles, basketballs, and a swing set. It's no perfect ocean view, but it's home, it's outside, and it's ours. No matter the state of my heart, God uses the porch moments to restore, refresh, and renew me. Whether I'm sitting out there, just me, God, and my Bible, or if I'm swinging with one of my kiddos, the fresh air and swaying motion refresh my heart and seem to lull me back into God's rhythm of grace again. The porch moments slow me down. Winter is always a tricky time for me to enjoy the porch. But if I'm wrapped up in enough blankets and have a hot cup of coffee, I can usually stand the cold for a few minutes. It's always worth it to soak in some porch moments for my heart.

Maybe the porch isn't quite your thing. Maybe there's another way you enjoy God's creation. But today I want you to remember the importance of taking time to get out in God's creation so He can minister to you through it. One of my favorite go-to books when I'm feeling a little soul weary is *If Mama Goes South, We're All Going with Her.* I love what the author, Lindsey O'Connor, says about getting outside:

So, "Girl, get outside!" Find a way to add half an hour of air and sun to your life daily and see how much better you feel. Walk. Garden. Sit on the porch to read, work, or process the mail. . . . Grab the sun screen, shades, and a hat and avoid baking in the sun, but do expose yourself to God's wonderful tonic and elixir daily, even if just for fifteen minutes. The fresh air and healing properties of the sun are a quick, easy, free way to keep Mama from going south. We just need to remember to accept this gift from God.[1]

Mamas or not, we all need God's healing and the calming effects of His creation. I know it sounds simple to step outside and soak in the beauty of God's creation, but today, I hope we embrace this gift from God in a deeper way.

My young sons and I often talk about how God must have had so much fun creating the world. He intentionally created such interesting creatures (think doodlebugs, giraffes, and butterflies). He went to so much trouble to create a vast array of different kinds of flowers (roses, buttercups, and dandelions). He threw in seasons so creation would never look quite the same from day to day. The story of creation is the very first thing God gives us in His Word (see Genesis 1–2). He took the earth, which was "formless and empty" (1:2 NIV), and created light, day, night, water, land, sky, earth, plants, trees, seasons, sun, moon, stars, living creatures, and such. He took nothing and filled the earth with beauty, as if maybe He was preparing it for His masterpieces—humans. He didn't have to make the earth beautiful, but He wanted to.

God's creation points us to Him. We can't help but stare at creation in awe. We can't help but be amazed. "The heavens declare the glory of God; the skies proclaim the work of his hands. Day after day they pour forth speech; night after night they reveal knowledge. They have no speech, they use no words; . . . their voice goes out into all the earth, their words to the ends of the world" (Ps. 19:1–4 NIV). But as you and I both know, we are busy gals, and we can easily forget the importance of taking a few moments each day to gaze at God's creation. I love what Romans 1:20 says: "For his invisible attributes, that is, his eternal power and divine nature, have been clearly seen since the creation of the world, being understood through what he has made." Soaking in God's creation sets our souls right, reminding us that God is present. I know it's easy to grow numb to the beauty of creation as we go about our busy lives, and that's okay—that's real life. But what if today we take note that God uses His creation to refresh, renew, and restore us? He uses it simply to bless us, to love on us, and to let us know He's real. God whispers to our hearts through creation, convincing us He is present.

I love Job 38, in which the Lord speaks to Job about the wonders of His creation. Here are verses 4–12, 16:

> Where were you when I laid the earth's foundation?
>   Tell me, if you understand.
> Who marked off its dimensions? Surely you know!
>   Who stretched a measuring line across it?
> On what were its footings set,
>   or who laid its cornerstone—
> while the morning stars sang together
>   and all the angels shouted for joy?
> Who shut up the sea behind the doors
>   when it burst forth from the womb,
> when I made the clouds its garment
>   and wrapped it in thick darkness,

when I fixed limits for it
and set its doors and bars in place,
when I said, "This far you may come and no farther;
here is where your proud waves halt"?
Have you ever given orders to the morning,
or shown the dawn its place. . . .
Have you journeyed to the springs of the sea
or walked in the recesses of the deep? (NIV)

Creation convinces us of His presence. And the beauty breathes refreshment into our hearts because we are reminded that the God who holds creation together holds us. The God who marked off the boundaries of the oceans lives in us. The God who formed beauty out of darkness forms beauty out of what feels messy in us. As we look to Him, specifically by taking some quiet moments to ponder His creation, He pours beauty, joy, and praise into our hearts. As we gaze on Him and His creation, our roots of faith grow deeper.

So today take some porch moments or any kind of moments outside in God's creation. Breathe in the beauty of His work. Whatever your view—whether you're oceanside, mountainside, or overlooking a busy city—look for the wonders of creation right outside your window. Ponder the beauty of God's gift of creation to us, and let Him minister to your soul in a way that only He can. This pondering forces us to slow our pace. So sink into a slower pace today, and watch what God does in your soul. Let the wonders of God's creation refresh, renew, and restore your heart.

GARDEN MOMENTS
for Your Soul

How you can take in God's creation today? What do your porch moments look like?

....

....

....

....

....

How does gazing on God's creation minister to your soul?

....

....

....

....

....

· · · · · · · · · · · **Pray** · · · · · · · · · · ·

Father God, thank You for Your beautiful creation and how You use it to minister to Your sons and daughters. Thank You for going to all the trouble to make our earth gorgeous with its vast spectrum of colors, creatures, and landscapes. Thank You for a day to focus on the gift of Your creation. Help me use my own porch moments to ponder You and Your creation. Help me remember to get outside and soak in all the beauty. Refresh, renew, and restore me through it. Help me remember to soak in the view of creation outside my own window daily so that I am able to slow my pace and become more aware of Your presence. Thank You for the beautiful gift of Your creation.

DAY 20

Dig into Your Work

> *May you see today that your work can be worship. Every task, every errand, and everything you do can be something you do with the Lord and for the Lord. May you dig into your work today as you see it as a gift from God—your special assignment from Him and another way you can love God with all your heart, soul, and mind (see Matt. 22:37).*

Work wholeheartedly, fearing the Lord. Whatever you do, do it from the heart, as something done for the Lord and not for people.

COLOSSIANS 3:22–23

WE DISCUSSED EARLIER how retreats with God are a kind of dance of drawing close to the Lord and then going out again and returning to our day—out into the world doing what we do. Today we are going to talk about digging into our work and changing our perspective of it. When we look at our day as an opportunity to worship God with all that we do, it brings joy to our perspective and lifts our spirits as we go about our work. This shift can be a game changer in our lives.

A couple of years ago, my husband and I hired a landscape crew to beautify our backyard. They installed flower beds, brought in loads of fresh soil, and carefully planted each and every new plant from one end of the yard to the other. I spent a lot of time watching the team at work. They arrived early each day dressed for the job and always right on time. And from the time they arrived to the time the sun went down, they worked hard. They dug into their work (quite literally). It impressed me and stirred something within me to want to work that hard. It brought to the surface some of the distractions that I felt were disrupting my everyday life. This crew inspired me to dig into my own work, whether that was parenting three boys, folding laundry, or diving into my current writing project. To stay with it. To get lost in it. To work undistracted. To be grateful and to go all in. They were doing the deep work of cultivating the soil and preparing the beds so the plants and flowers would fully flourish. I couldn't help but see a beautiful picture of how God wants us to dig into our assignments with His help so that He can grow something beautiful from it. And in a day and age when we carry so much mentally—with our to-do lists, information at our fingertips, emails, you name it—it's hard to dive deep into special assignments from God with full focus. I love how this landscape crew took such pride in their progress. They worked really hard, and I'm sure they rested really hard when they went home.

155

Sometimes we can fall into the trap of seeing our assignments from God, whatever it may be, as drudgery. We get caught in the daily grind and coast through our day instead of digging fully into the task before us. But I think if we looked at our days as a way to worship God, then this could flip our perspective and renew our energy and passion. Our time with God is vital to our relationship with Him, but it doesn't stop there. When we step out of our quiet time, we don't have to leave God there to go about our business, only to return to Him the next day. Instead, He can go with us. I love what David says in Psalm 27:4: "I have asked one thing from the LORD; it is what I desire: to dwell in the house of the LORD all the days of my life, gazing on the beauty of the LORD and seeking him in his temple." David was expressing that he wanted to experience God all day every day. When we view our work as a way to experience God, our whole day becomes a time of worship. As we invite God into our work and do our tasks wholeheartedly for Him, we reap the sweet rewards of satisfaction, contentment, and joy. Second Corinthians 9:6 says it this way: "The person who sows sparingly will also reap sparingly, and the person who sows generously will also reap generously." Now, this verse is speaking to giving specifically, but I think we can apply it to the way we live as well. When we sow deep roots of hard work with an attitude of worshiping God, we reap the rewards and build a closer relationship with Him.

Back in our verse for the day Paul calls us to "work wholeheartedly," "from the heart" and "for the Lord." And I love this little tidbit: "whatever you do." So whether we're doing a job, running an errand, performing a chore, or act-ing creatively, Paul urges us to work from our hearts—with passion and joy. What grabbed my heart as I watched that landscape crew work so hard was that they showed passion. They embraced what God had given them to do and did it wholeheartedly. They didn't complain. Their work ethic was a beautiful example to me. Psalm 16:5–6 says,

> Lord, you are my portion
> and my cup of blessing;
> you hold my future.
> The boundary lines have fallen for me
> in pleasant places;
> indeed, I have a beautiful inheritance.

The lot or boundary lines God has given each of us in life are good. That doesn't mean we don't hope for different circumstances or dream of doing different work. But I believe God wants us to dig into our work right where we are and worship Him through it. In an age when everything is instantaneous, we can forget the value of hard, deep, slow work. There is beauty in embracing the process, of long and faithful work, of sowing richly.

When we do our work for God instead of just for ourselves or others, our motivation changes. When we own the work God has given us and believe He's set our feet on the path we are on, we go about our work differently. When we see that every aspect of our day is what God is developing in us as part of His master plan for our lives and see that there's value in the lessons we are learning in our current season, our passion for our work grows.

What does it look like to worship God with our work? It's simply the idea that we bring Him into whatever we're doing, knowing He's with us. We ask for His help and choose to have a great attitude. Sometimes I get caught up in compartmentalizing my work—parenting in this box, writing in this box, chores over in this box, ministry-related stuff over here—and the more "spiritual" stuff feels more, well, spiritual. But 1 Corinthians 10:31 says, "So whether you eat or drink or whatever you do, do it all for the glory of God" (NIV). Instead of compartmentalizing our lives, what if we did it *all* for the glory of God? What if we looked at doing the dishes as just as sacred as something more "spiritual"? What if we saw everything as spiritual? What if we chose a great attitude and happy heart, as I like to say to my boys, in all that we do? How might it affect others? How might it affect us?

There's nothing quite as inspiring as seeing someone enjoy their work, whatever that work is, without complaining. They do what's right in front of them with joy and peace. And they seem truly happy about it! As daughters of Christ, we can dig into our work with the same kind of gusto. And when we do, I believe it will beautifully affect our outlook on some of the things in our day that maybe feel mundane.

In Genesis 1, God sends the man and woman off with His blessing. "God blessed them, and God said to them, 'Be fruitful, multiply, fill the earth, and subdue it'" (v. 28). God designed us to work, create, and be productive. Ephesians 2:10 says, "For we are his workmanship, created in Christ Jesus for good works, which God prepared ahead of time for us to do." This is a reminder that God has specific work for each of us to complete. And day to day, it's not always going to feel glamorous or fruitful. Some days it's going to feel frustrating and we will wonder if it's worth it. Some days it's going to feel like no one sees or appreciates our work. But God sees you. He sees your behind-the-scenes effort. And He wants you to work hard for Him and with Him.

We typically can't wait to see the results of our efforts. But when we dig into the process, appreciate the tasks God has given us to do, and worship God in all we do, we will discover the beauty. I love what author Mark Batterson says in *Draw the Circle*: "We need to work like it depends on us, but we also need to pray like it depends on God."[1] This is a beautiful reminder that prayer and working hard for God go hand in hand. It's not realistic to only pray and not work hard. And at the same time, God doesn't want us to work hard but never lean on Him in prayer. He wants us to work hard and pray about our work. And when we do, that is when our work is most fruitful.

I hope today you will be encouraged to dig into your work. I hope you know God has created and wired you for specific works (see Ps. 139). I hope you will gain a sense of purpose as you embrace your work and talk to God through prayer. I pray you'll see every day as an opportunity to glorify your Maker in everything you do. And I hope you discover the treasure of new springs of joy rising in your heart as you worship God with your efforts and enjoy His company as you do so. "This is the day that the LORD has made; let us rejoice and be glad in it" (Ps. 118:24 ESV). Today is a gift. Your work, whatever that may be, is a gift. Know God is producing fruit through you.

GARDEN MOMENTS
for Your Soul

How can you worship God with your work?

....

....

....

....

....

In what ways do you feel encouraged that everything you do can be an opportunity to worship God?

....

....

....

....

....

· · · · · · · · · ·   *Pray*   · · · · · · · ·

Lord, thank You for the work You've given me to do. Help me see it with a fresh perspective. Help me see that You've blessed me with this job right in front of me.

Help me dig in, own it, and work hard in it with You and for You. Help me lace my efforts with prayer, trusting You with the fruit. Help me embrace the process, and diligently tend to the tasks You've given me. Help me see my whole day as an opportunity to glorify You. Help me continue on, both when my work feels significant and when it feels like no one sees me. Remind me that You see me. Thank You for establishing the work of my hands. Give me a new appreciation for the jobs, roles, and assignments You've given me.

Tend the In-Between Moments

> *Know today that God is as close as your right hand. "I always let the LORD guide me. Because he is at my right hand, I will not be shaken" (Ps. 16:8). He's in all your moments through-out the day. Find Him in the in-between moments, trust He's with you, and know a deeper sense of His presence.*

Look carefully then how you walk
. . . making the best use of the time.

EPHESIANS 5:15–16 ESV

YESTERDAY WE TALKED about worshiping God with our whole day, and today I want to talk specifically about the in-between waiting moments. We wait in line, wait in traffic, wait for our favorite show to come on, wait to go out on a date, wait to receive the good news we've been hoping for, or wait for a friend to call us back. In other words, life isn't one exciting, flashy, and glamorous moment after another. No, life is a beautiful mix of the glorious, joy-filled moments; the everyday funny, happy, and restful moments; the practical real-life moments; as well as the in-between waiting moments. Life is how we spend our moments. And too often when we get bored, impatient, or just kind of stuck in the grind, or when we feel that deep inner angst of what to do with the restlessness, we may be tempted to run to things that don't necessarily feed our hearts. Instead, we run to things that deplete us. Then our in-between moments become depleting moments.

Today's verse in Ephesians comes from a section in chapter 5 in which Paul is encouraging the people of Ephesus to pay attention to how they are living the Christian life. He writes,

> Pay careful attention, then, to how you live—not as unwise people but as wise—making the most of the time, because the days are evil. So don't be foolish, but understand what the Lord's will is. . . . Be filled by the Spirit: speaking to one another in psalms, hymns, and spiritual songs, singing and making music with your heart to the Lord, giving thanks always for everything to God the Father in the name of our Lord Jesus Christ. (vv. 15–20)

I love Paul's call for us to pay careful attention to how we live. In a sense, he's urging us not to waste our time. He also gives us some practical ways to help make better use of our time. Paul wants us to be aware of how we're spending our time and to make the best of it.

What if we reclaimed our in-between moments as opportunities to curl up to the only One who can truly satisfy our thirsty hearts? What if, when we feel those thirsty moments, we drank from the presence of God instead of filling them up with stuff that doesn't fulfill? What if we tuned in to God in each in-between moment and asked, "God, how do you want me to use these few minutes of downtime?" Maybe He will lead us to open our Bibles, or to be still and be aware of His presence, or to love on our child who is sitting across the room from us, or to think on a verse He showed us earlier in the day. Or maybe, like Paul alludes to, He will lead us to take a moment to check in with the Spirit, or sing a song in our hearts to God, or encourage a friend. What if instead of checking out, we checked in with Him?

God is present in all our moments, including every in-between moment. I tend to look for Him in those big moments, and yes, He's there, but He's also in the small moments. He can redeem all our in-between moments, loving on us and speaking to us. He wants to let us know that He's there. This is abiding in God's presence all day long. And it becomes this dance of walking with Him, knowing Him, and tuning in to Him. Writer Annie Dillard says it this way: "How we spend our days is, of course, how we spend our lives."[1] That statement wakes me up a bit! I believe our in-between moments can bless, fuel, and nurture us if we tend them well. They can bless others too. How do we want to spend our lives? Growing and truly living abundantly. So we must pay attention to these quiet intervals in our day and choose to be intentional about how we spend them.

It's really a challenge to tend our in-between moments well because they come at us unexpectedly and all the time. But just being aware and having the desire to tend these moments well is half the battle. God helps us in this detail of life too. "I will bless the Lord who counsels me . . . I always let the Lord guide me" (Ps. 16:7–8). And it's absolutely worth it! We can ask the Lord to "teach us to number our days carefully so that we may develop wisdom in our hearts" (Ps. 90:12). Imagine the gift of redeemed in-between moments. Imagine the fruit God can bear in you as you tend your time with His help. Imagine the growth. I know it feels easier at times to run to other things that aren't necessarily bad (our phones, the news, the TV, the computer, etc.), but how different might we feel deep in our core if we chose life-giving things instead (simply checking in with God through prayer, tuning in to His Word when we have a quiet moment, singing a song to the Lord, sending an encouraging text to a friend, a moment to be still and know He is God)? How might tending our in-between moments change us?

Part of tending our in-between moments requires that we be prepared for them. Maybe keep a pocket-size Bible in your purse or a journal and pen close by. Store your phone out of sight so it's not the first thing you run to. Set yourself up for success. Take some moments to think about your in-between moments and how, with God's help and leading, you can better tend them.

Today, when one of those in-between moments comes, pause a second and see how God might want to check in with you. He's so very present in your life. It's tempting to fill up our in-between moments with things that deplete us, but when we run to God instead, He satisfies our hearts like nothing else in the world can. Filling our in-between moments with God's presence affects our hearts in the best kind of way, which in turn affects the rest of our day and our whole lives.

GARDEN MOMENTS
for Your Soul

Take a moment to reflect on how you typically spend your in-between moments and what it would be like to tend them in a more life-giving way.

....

....

....

....

....

What encourages you most about tending your in-between moments?

....

....

....

....

....

....

· · · · · · · · · · **Pray** · · · · · · · · ·

Lord, thank You for being present in all my moments. Help me better tend my in-between moments. Show me how I have been spending my minutes, and teach me how to number my days. Help me believe that filling this time by checking in with You is far more fulfilling and satisfying than anything else. Let Your Spirit guide me in better tending every moment of the day. I long to live a fruitful, growing, and flourishing life. Thank You for Your grace when I don't tend my moments well. Thank You that Your love for me never changes according to what I do or don't do. Give me fresh motivation to know You deeper still and to invite You into every moment of my day.

DAY 22

Make Room for the Spirit

> *Today choose the Spirit-led life, because where the Spirit of the Lord is, there is freedom (see 2 Cor. 3:17). Let the Spirit lead your heart, guide your thoughts, and direct your steps. Instead of a try-hard life, embrace the Spirit's work in you. Tune in. Listen. And discover deeper joy, fuller life, and true peace as you walk in step with the Spirit.*

For those who live according to the flesh set their minds on the things of the flesh, but those who live according to the Spirit set their minds on the things of the Spirit. For to set the mind on the flesh is death, but to set the mind on the Spirit is life and peace.

ROMANS 8:5–6 (ESV)

THE SPIRIT-LED LIFE can feel a bit mysterious. We easily grow accustomed to our day-to-day rhythms and routines, and we almost go on autopilot at times. We make our lists, set our calendars, and plow into our days, but what if we are missing out on a sweeter peace and joy? We know we should tune in to the Spirit and listen to His whispers, but we either forget or it feels hard to know if we're doing it right.

I've known about the Holy Spirit for as long as I can remember, but I feel like I am still learning every day what it looks like to walk by the Spirit versus the flesh. The moments when I feel truly connected with the Spirit are the best. It's like I feel God's presence right there in my midst. But other days it's like I forget to intentionally tune in, which leaves me feeling a bit off.

Recently one Sunday morning my little family was sitting in our usual row at church. We sang several worship songs and then the kiddos were released to go to their classes. I scooted closer to Brian and held my coffee cup close, ready for the day's message. Our pastor preached about the Spirit-filled life, and something he said seemed to wake up my heart. Something clicked. He talked about how we have to be vigilant and intentional about setting our minds on the Spirit. We have to choose to do so. It doesn't come naturally. Our natural bent is to operate in our flesh. But for us to experience the life and peace the Spirit offers, we must choose to set our minds on the things of the Spirit. I knew this, but I had failed to remember. So I grabbed a piece of paper and scribbled notes as fast as I could because I didn't want to forget again. I didn't want to forget that connecting with the Spirit requires awareness. I didn't want to forget that the Spirit-filled life is where peace and life and freedom meet—and that's where I wanted to be and stay.

Today I want us to see that setting our minds on the Spirit is an invitation to greater peace and joy. I love how Hannah Whitall Smith puts it this way: "In a thousand ways He makes this offer of oneness with Himself to every believer. But all do not say 'Yes' to Him. Other loves and other interests seem to them too precious to be cast aside. They do not miss heaven because of this. But they do miss an unspeakable joy. We don't miss heaven by walking in the flesh or tuning out the Spirit either intentionally or unintentionally, but we do miss an *unspeakable joy.*"[1]

If you're tired of feeling like you're missing God, a deeper joy, or more or abundant life, Paul has a sweet secret for you that could change everything. What if setting our minds on the Spirit is key? What if we got intentional about setting our minds on the Spirit? What if we became vigilant about making space in our days and our lives and our hearts for the Spirit to speak, lead, and guide us? What if we remembered each day that to choose the Spirit is to choose a life of sweeter intimacy with the Lord?

I want all of us to experience a connection to God on a daily basis. I think many of us want a closer relationship with Him. We want more of Him and more of His presence. Today I would like us to see that it does take some self-discipline to make space for God. It takes setting aside other things in order to know the best thing—God Himself. In a day and age when we have so many distractions—including emails, texts, social media, and television—making space can be challenging. This is what our enemy wants. He wants to keep us busy and distracted so he can turn our attention far away from God and the peace, joy, life, and freedom He offers. He wants us to take in all the digital information, emails, and newsfeed we can so we have no room left for God.

What if we became women on a mission to set our minds on the things of the Spirit? What if we laid down some boundaries for our phones or inboxes or whatever else is running our day and were fueled by the Spirit instead? What if we focused on following the Holy Spirit's lead?

Not only would we live purposeful lives, but we would live with deeper peace. We would discover an unspeakable joy as we protect that connection with our Savior every day. Nothing is worth breaking our connection to the True Vine. Daughter of Christ, He wants to spend time with you. He wants to lead you and whisper His love notes of truth and hope to you. But He needs you to turn down the volume of all the other noise. He needs you to quiet your heart so you can hear Him speak. It's not easy to turn down the noise of the world, but the peace and joy you will find in Him will make the choice worth it. Let the action of setting your mind on the Spirit be something you are intentional and vigilant about every day.

GARDEN MOMENTS
for Your Soul

What does it mean to you to set your mind on the things of the Spirit?

....

....

....

....

....

What's keeping you from living a Spirit-filled life?

....

....

....

....

· · · · · · · · · · **Pray** · · · · · · · · ·

Lord, I want to live a Spirit-filled life. I want to know the joy, freedom, and intimacy You offer through Your Spirit. Show me how to set my mind on the Spirit. Show me how to choose the Spirit over my flesh. Show me how to protect my connection with You from distractions. I choose You. I want all the life and peace You offer. Help me remember every day to be intentional and vigilant about walking with Your beautiful Spirit.

....

....

....

....

....

DAY 23

Light

May God's restoring light fill your heart as you lean in close to Him. May you feel the light of God's presence as you go about your day. Look to the One who is the giver of light and allow Him to brighten your heart from the inside out.

God is light, and there is absolutely no darkness in him.

1 JOHN 1:5

AS WE SLOW OUR PACE and savor quiet moments with the Lord, He brightens our hearts with His goodness, presence, and love. He is our light. Psalm 27:1 says, "The Lord is my light and my salvation—whom should I fear? The Lord is the stronghold of my life—whom should I dread?" In a world that can feel really dark at times, we can always have the hope of God in every moment. He keeps our hearts fully alive with the bright light of His constant presence. In Him, there is no darkness. Today let's stir up God's light in us as we remember that He is our constant source and our constant hope.

One click on the newsfeed or one check of the evening news can throw our hearts into a tailspin. There have been moments when I've curled up in bed after a busy day, ready to take a few moments to relax before I hit the pillow for the night, and instead of a good book or even a good show, I check the news. But most times, the shock of the next difficult story suppresses my joy, stirs up my angst, and makes me focus on the evil in our world. I'm sure you've felt it too. I go to bed feeling fearful or stressed instead of peaceful. It can feel like evil is winning. The joy of knowing God and that our eternity is secure seems to get outweighed by fear. So how do we keep the light of God stirred up in us and shining brightly in the midst of darkness?

Every February, I scatter hyacinth bean seed pods in sunny spots in our yard. Not much is needed to plant these—no shovel or garden gloves required. You can literally toss them in the soil, push some dirt on top of them with your foot, and they're good to go. As long as the pods get enough sun, they grow fast and furiously, blooming into gorgeous vines of purple flowers that resemble orchids. Because purple is my favorite color, these little pods have won my heart. I love watching them go from little dry pods to thriving plants. They really need a lot of light though to truly flourish. As long as they have the light of the sun and get plenty of it day to day, they bloom in all their meant-to-be glory. Without sun, they stay pods. I think the same is true of us. This is different from getting the light of the sunshine from the outdoors like we touched on earlier. Here I want us to see that we need to expose our hearts to the light of God's presence and His Word day to day in order to bloom in all our meant-to-be glory. We need God's light to overshadow the darkness around us so we can flourish and live without fear. We can keep that light stirred up by thinking about Him, opening our hearts to Him, keeping His Word close, and praying when we feel the darkness closing in.

I love what 1 John 1:4 says: "We are writing these things so that our joy may be complete." This verse encourages us to know God and all that we have in Him so that *our joy may be complete*. John recognized that knowing Him makes us happy, stirs up the light in us, and completes our joy. This implies that God wants us to know the fullness of Him. He wants us to be happy. He doesn't want us to live in fear. And so John goes on: "God is light, and there is absolutely no darkness in Him" (v. 5). It's so good for us to remember where to run when we feel the darkness of the world creeping up on us—toward the Light. God's light restores His peace back to our hearts. God's light exposes our fears and worries and brings our hearts back to a state of always having hope. "As for me, I will always have hope; I will praise you more and more" (Ps. 71:14 NIV).

Just like I can't explain how my little hyacinth bean seeds go from tiny pods to vines of purple flowers, I can't explain how or what God does in our hearts when we expose them to His light. "He lifted me out of the pit of despair, out of the mud and the mire. He set my feet on solid ground and steadied me as I walked along" (Ps. 40:2 NLT). If we run to Him when we feel fearful or when the darkness feels like it's winning, He pulls us out of the muck and back into His steady peace. He draws us away from the icky emotions of fear, worry, angst, and dread and toward His light again, which, in turn, lifts our spirits. I don't know how He does it, but He does it. Over and over again, He completes our joy. He pushes out the darkness so that more and more of His light can shine into our hearts. And just like those little pods, we need lots and lots of His light. The more the better. His light keeps us growing and flourishing.

It's not just the news and the darkness of the world that can suppress God's light in us. Our own insecurities and doubts about who we are, what we look like, and a million other little things can suppress the light. A discouraging thought, a negative outlook, a hurtful comment from somebody—the small things can deplete our joy. This brings us back around again to the importance of guarding our hearts. What are we focusing on? What are we watching or reading or looking at? It's so important to tend our souls. I love the King James Version of Deuteronomy 4:9: "Only take heed to thyself, and keep thy soul diligently." This is a reminder to keep watch over the door of our hearts and souls. Be careful about the thoughts or lies that are coming through. The smallest things can cause our souls to feel a little off. The smallest doubt, fear, or insecurity can suppress the light of God within us. We can expose our souls to the light of God's presence and allow it to uncover anything that is causing us to wilt instead of flourish. When we make God the center of our lives, the stronghold, our everything, we have constant hope and constant light. It doesn't mean we won't ever experience darkness. But we always have a way back to full joy. We will always know where to run.

Sometimes taking that step toward God and to the light of His presence and Word can feel hard. I seem to grow forgetful and run to something else instead of God. I busy myself with a chore or just turn off the light, roll over, and go to sleep as I try not to think about the scary world we live in. Or I escape into a good show or my phone to numb the fear or anxiety I feel. We all run to different things to get away from the darkness and angst. But today let's remind ourselves that when we run to God instead, we find all that we need. We find relief from the fear, peace in the storm, joy we were made for. He lights us up again.

"Consider me and answer, Lord my God. Restore brightness to my eyes" (Ps. 13:3). He will gladly restore the brightness to your eyes. I can't really say how He does it, but He will do it. He will take those things lingering in your heart that are causing you to feel stuck or in despair, and He will draw you back into His beautiful light. He will pour His light into your heart, restoring you back to full joy. "You reveal the path of life to me; in your presence is abundant joy; at your right hand are eternal pleasures" (Ps. 16:11). He longs for us to stay on His path and not get sucked into the path the world can lure us onto, which is one of fear, worry, dread, and darkness. As we learn this dance of walking moment to moment with God, we will know His *abundant joy*. We will know His *eternal pleasures*—this well of joy, hope, and light that we have constant access to.

I don't know what's suppressing God's light in you today, but I can tell you what usually suppresses it in me. Typically, it's several small things that add up to one big, heavy load of oppression. It's the silly things. The small insecurities that I can't seem to throw off. It's the lies the enemy has caused me to believe or the lurking darkness of the world we live in that he uses to try to get me down. But like you, I want to live with bright eyes and a bright heart. I want to shine in a world that's hurting and craving God's light. I want to live and walk in the light (see 1 John 1:7). So while I don't do it perfectly, because this gal can be quite forgetful, I try to remember where my hope comes from: "My help comes from the LORD, the Maker of heaven and earth" (Ps. 121:2 NIV). When I get a bit caddywonk in my soul, I remind myself to quickly return my attention to God. And when I do, when I simply come to Him with whatever is suppressing the light in me, He does His thing. He brightens my heart again. He restores my light with His light. He shakes off the dust in me. "Shake off your dust; rise up, sit enthroned, Jerusalem. Free yourself from the chains on your neck, Daughter Zion" (Isa. 52:2 NIV). He exposes the fears, lies, or insecurities that are weighing down my heart. Over and over again, He faithfully ministers to me with the light of His beautiful presence and Word. And He will faithfully do the same for you as you turn to Him. You can trust Him to pull you back into His light. This is the work of the Master Gardener of your heart. Remember, we always have hope—both eternally and in this earth-life. Because we have God, we always have light and hope.

GARDEN MOMENTS
for Your Soul

What fears, doubts, insecurities, or darkness are oppressing God's light in you today?

....

....

....

....

....

How do you typically handle these moments, and how can you get your soul to God instead?

....

....

....

....

....

· · · · · · · · · ·   **Pray**   · · · · · · · · ·

God, thank You for being our constant source of light and hope. Thank You for promising to turn my darkness into light. Thank You for bringing the sun out in my heart to experience the well of joy I can know in You. And Lord, when I forget where to run to find freedom from the weight of darkness, whisper a reminder to run to You. Teach me to look to You when I feel darkness winning. Thank You for taking what feels dark and heavy and hard and turning it into joy again—over and over. You are faithful. You are beautiful. You are light. Be my light every day and be my source of joy. Make my joy complete as I bring every hint of darkness lurking in my heart to You. Make my heart shine for You.

DAY 24
Well-Watered

When your soul feels thirsty, run to the well of God's presence. This is where your thirst is quenched. This is where your soul finds satisfaction. Keep the roots of your faith watered with God's Word and presence.

As a deer longs for flowing streams,
so I long for you, God.
———
PSALM 42:1

TODAY WE'RE GOING TO TALK about soul-thirst. We've been talking about the state of our souls quite a bit, and all these topics can seem to overlap each other at times. I think we're learning that all in all, God is the One we want to train our hearts to run to. So while today's topic may seem a little bit repetitive, I think it's worth rehearsing truth to our hearts over and over again. Maybe we will see soul-thirst in a fresh, new way, and I hope today is encouraging to you.

We all know what it feels like to be physically thirsty. We carry around our water bottles and work hard to stay hydrated. We can typically tell when we need water. Our throats feel dry, our energy may be low, and we experience a thirst that we really can't ignore. We operate better physically when we are hydrated. As a mama, I struggle to make sure my boys are hydrating with water instead of chocolate milk, apple juice, or Capri Sun. Convincing them of the goodness of water is a bit tricky. They want the sweet stuff for sure! And as a writer, I could drink coffee all day. It seems that the flow of words and the flow of coffee go hand-in-hand. So I have to be extra diligent about making sure I make room for the pure water my body needs. In the same way, soul-thirst is that feeling of needing something we can't define. It's noticing our souls are off. It's recognizing we feel dry and empty. Our souls thirst for the pure flow of God's Word and His living water. We operate best when our spiritual thirst is quenched in God alone.

In Psalm 42, the psalmist seems to be preaching to his own heart. "Why, my soul, are you so dejected? Why are you in such turmoil? Put your hope in God, for I will still praise him, my Savior and my God" (v. 5). He's reminding himself to put his hope back in God. And just as a deer follows a stream to get the water it desperately needs to survive, we can run to the stream of God's living water so we can thrive, not just survive. But sometimes we must preach to our own hearts. As we begin to notice when our souls feel thirsty, we can remind ourselves to get our hearts to God. Kind of like we talked about yesterday, God is our source for everything. We must remember that the well of God is where we find a well of satisfaction. Our souls were created to be satisfied in God alone.

Recently I stepped outside my front door to check my mail. As I walked past this one pot of pansies, they nearly stopped me in my tracks. Due to my busy week, I had not taken the time to water them, so they were dry, wilting, and looked just plain sad. I made a mental note to water them as soon as possible. I grabbed the water pitcher on my way inside and filled it up at the sink. A few hours later, I watered the pansies and went about my day. The next day, I stepped outside again to check the mail and walked past the same pot of flowers. Their flourishing beauty stopped me in my tracks. I couldn't believe how vibrant they looked just a day after a good soak. And I thought right then and there, that's what God does for our souls. When we come to Him weary, dry, and on empty, He waters us. He pours His living water deep into our souls and brings us back to true flourishing.

Let's take a look at the story of when Jesus greets the Samaritan woman at the well (see John 4:1–26).

> Jesus said, "Everyone who drinks from this water will get thirsty again. But whoever drinks from the water that I will give him will never get thirsty again. In fact, the water I will give him will become a well of water springing up in him for eternal life." (vv. 13–14)

Here Jesus was inviting this imperfect, everyday woman to know the satisfaction, both eternally and presently, of knowing God. This verse shows us that Jesus satisfies the internal soul-thirst we feel as well as the eternal thirst to be right with God. The Samaritan woman was not more righteous than the next gal walking to the well. In fact, from what we can tell, she may have had a difficult past. But Jesus offers His living water despite her past. He offered the very thing she needed and what she may not have even known she needed—eternal salvation and satisfaction for her soul. I love verses 25–26. Take a look at them: "The woman said to him, 'I know that the Messiah is coming' (who is called Christ). 'When he comes, he will explain everything to us.' Jesus told her, 'I, the one speaking to you, am he.'"

The answer to her deep soul-thirst was right in front of her, and she didn't realize it. And it makes me think about how many times the answer to our own soul-thirst, Jesus, is right in front of or right with us and we don't even realize it. We look around for something to satisfy us when He is right here in our midst. We run to other things to fill us instead of running to the One who longs to quench our thirst. We run to our own solutions, trying hard to fix our feelings or change the state of our souls, when the remedy to our dry souls is present. Today let's look at this soul-thirst as a gift. Our souls were designed to crave God. And God designed our souls to get thirsty when they need more of Him. We tend to look at soul-thirst as a bad thing. And it can certainly feel like a bad thing when we are in a dry moment or season. But what if we looked at that thirst as an arrow pointing us to God?

During this writing season, I definitely felt what many writers feel as they are working to finish their manuscript: dry, empty, and out of words. There were moments when I felt like I had nothing left. Inside, I was wilting a little. But I didn't want to admit it. I was feeling a teeny bit stressed about finishing the manuscript. I felt God nudge my heart to step away for a bit and allow Him to fill me back up because my soul was a little dehydrated. So I did just that. I set my work aside and let my soul breathe and rest in God for a while. And later the words I couldn't find before came flowing out. He reminded me that He's where my help comes from. He's my source. He's the well of satisfaction my soul needs. And in the same way, today I want us to see that our soul-thirst is an arrow pointing us to the One who satisfies. Every time we feel depleted, we can make a choice to see it as soul-thirst and get our souls quickly to God. Instead of pushing through or striving, we can rest in God and allow Him to refill us with His living water. There will be times when we have to work hard and push through. There will be moments that call for digging deep and working hard. But when it comes to a gal's soul being plain thirsty for God, she will find a well of refreshment when she listens to that thirst and runs to God.

A gal doesn't have to operate on empty. She always has the Living Water right there in her midst. But she must choose Him. She must believe Jesus is right there with her. And most times she will find that the refreshment begins the moment she draws from the well of God's presence and Word. The moment she chooses God over other stuff, her soul feels the effects. The spring of water from within begins to flow more freely, and suddenly she's on her way again, fresh and filled up.

Gals, we are the ones who must tend our souls and get them to God. We must choose to keep our souls well hydrated in God. And throughout our busy lives, sometimes we get so overloaded that we forget the source of our hydration. Or we think we will get our souls to God when we have more time. Or we believe this other thing will satisfy us, at least for a little bit. But as we preach to our own hearts today that God offers a constant supply of deep soul satisfaction, may we be spurred on to choose Him when we feel dry and empty. May we know His presence in a deeper way as we begin to recognize our soul-thirst and get our souls to God.

And know that His source of replenishment never runs dry. He always has more to give you. He never grows weary. He's always available to fill you up. No one else and nothing else can fill you up the way He can. I know we will still naturally run to other things or even lean on people to fill us back up again, but I hope today we are encouraged to run directly to God and to see that He is the one true source of nourishment for a thirsty soul. Next time you feel that soul-thirst, take a moment to follow the arrow to God's presence. And expect refreshment—the sweetest refreshment.

GARDEN MOMENTS
for Your Soul

In what ways has your soul felt thirsty lately?

....

....

....

....

How has God met you in your soul-thirst?

....

....

....
....
....
....
....

· · · · · · · · · · **Pray** · · · · · · · · · ·

Lord, thank You for being the One who replenishes me when I feel weary. Thank You for being my constant source of refreshment. Lord, help me remember to run to You instead of to other things or people. Help me remember that You are all I need to flourish and feel satisfied. Like the woman at the well finally saw that You were right there in her midst, help me see that You are right here with me in the everyday moments. Help me realize that You are available every moment of the day. And help me run to You when my soul feels thirsty. Thank You for the living water You provide for my soul, both eternally and presently. May I always run to You.

....
....
....
....
....

DAY 25

Grow in Grace

> *You don't have to transform yourself. Day by day, you are growing in grace. God will do the transforming work. He will produce the fruit in you. You don't have to strive, prove yourself, or reach some unattainable state of perfection. You can rest, cease striving, and let Him do His transforming work in you. So much more grace is available to you than you could ever imagine. Grace to be. Grace to grow.*

We all, with unveiled faces, are looking as in a mirror at the glory of the Lord and are being transformed into the same image from glory to glory; this is from the Lord who is the Spirit.

2 CORINTHIANS 3:18

KNOW THAT GOD SEES YOU. He sees your heart, your soul, your emotions, your dreams. He sees it all. He sees you. You don't have to have it all together for Him. You don't have to try to be better than you are. You don't have to try to be superwoman. You can be you. He wants you to be you. He wants you to know that your heart, your soul, your emotions, your dreams—they're all beautiful to Him. You're beautiful to Him. Sweet one, He's carefully tending your heart. He's guiding your steps. He's walking with you through this dance of life. He's got you. He's growing you into the woman He created you to be, but you don't have to do the growing—He'll do it. Today let's talk about what it means to grow in grace.

Today's verse is from 2 Corinthians 3 in which Paul is writing about the glorious news of the new covenant. He's comparing the restrictive ways of the old covenant to the freeing, grace-filled ways of the new. He brings in the topic of the Spirit with these words: "Now the Lord is the Spirit, and where the Spirit of the Lord is, there is freedom" (v. 17). He talks about how as we look to God, not through a veil and not through a priest, we reflect the glory of the Lord and in turn are transformed to be more like Him. And he notes that "this is from the Lord who is the Spirit" (v. 18). This is all the Spirit's work. We have been talking a lot about growing, flourishing, and blossoming as we draw close to the Lord, and today I want us to remember that all of that comes from God. All the transformation and growth we long for is God's work in us. While we can certainly be intentional about creating space in our lives and hearts for more of God like we've been discussing, may we never forget it's the Spirit's work. May we always remember that it's by God's grace that we grow. We can let go of trying hard to grow and trust the Spirit's work inside us.

I remember some advice a more experienced ballet dancer once gave me right in the middle of ballet class. She said, "You don't have to work so hard." That was crazy talk to me! I had no idea what she meant at the time. I was working as hard as I could to be the best ballet dancer I could possibly be. I was working my muscles, sweating profusely, fighting through the pain of tendonitis, and often driven by the pressure to reach perfection in my movement. And that dancer's advice was basically to stop working so hard. I was a bit confused in that moment.

Years and years later, I think I get it. Dancing, while it takes much intention, intense training, and focus, also takes letting go. Dancing is supposed to be fun, but when I was making it about pressure, pain, and pushing my body to the max, I lost my spark. I lost the reason I loved to dance. I lost the dance in my dancing, if you will. This brings me to our desire to grow in life. We can easily fall into performance mode. Life becomes a grind of working, striving, pushing, and pressing into the pressures we feel. But I'm learning that Jesus offers a totally different way (see Matt. 11:28–30). He actually wants to put the dancing back into our living so that we can enjoy our living. "I perceived that there is nothing better for them than to be joyful and to do good as long as they live" (Eccles. 5:14 ESV). We don't have to try so hard to grow. Instead, we can be so dependent on Him that we can lean back and enjoy the ride. I'm not exactly sure what that looks like. The dancer in me wants a perfect order of things, a perfect formula of what that looks like fleshed out. But the deep-down little girl in me who remembers what it is like to dance across the stage for no other reason than the sheer enjoyment of it echoes in my heart to keep seeking Jesus and to lean back in His grace. Because Jesus makes life a dance. Not a grind. Not a constant toiling. Not a striving ladder of effort. And He's calling us to get back to dancing life with Him. He's calling us to let go of the try-hard life and embrace the grace-filled life.

The apostle Peter also calls us to grow in grace: "But grow in the grace and knowledge of our Lord and Savior Jesus Christ" (2 Pet. 3:18). This reminds me of Zechariah 4:6: "Not by strength or by might, but by my Spirit." It doesn't mean we don't work hard, and it doesn't mean we don't show a little grit at times. But it's a reminder that we grow in grace, day by day, trusting the Spirit's work inside us. Ephesians 3:16–19 says, "I [Paul] pray . . . that Christ may dwell in your hearts through faith. I pray that you, being rooted and firmly established in love, may be able to comprehend with all the saints what is the length and width, height and depth of God's love, and to know Christ's love that surpasses knowledge, so that you may be filled with all the fullness of God." This verse shows us that as we root ourselves in God's love, we will be able to be filled with the fullness of God. And I believe there's a beautiful connection between being rooted in God's love and growing in grace. Instead of striving to grow, we can focus on God's love for us, trusting His Spirit in us to do the growing. Remember the vine and branches analogy? "I am the vine; you are the branches. The one who remains in me and I in him produces much fruit, because you can do nothing without me" (John 15:5). Growth is a natural result of being with God and deeply connected to Him. According to Ephesians 2:8, "For you are saved by grace through faith, and this is not from yourselves; it is God's gift." As we trust God's Spirit to work in us, He transforms. And this is all a gift.

Leaning back and allowing the Spirit to work from within us can feel tricky. I often catch myself in striving mode—trying to hold things together, work things out, push through, and make things happen. Or I attempt to be a better version of myself, forgetting that I don't have to try so hard. There's something magnetic about watching a ballerina who makes dancing appear effortless. It's as though she doesn't have to try, she just dances. She doesn't force the beauty; her dancing is just beautiful.

I was watching an episode of *American Idol* recently, and one of the judges told this one gifted singer that her singing was effortless. He also went on to note that when a singer has to try so hard, something is wrong. Something about singing should come from within—and be natural. I couldn't get his comment out of my mind in relation to how we live. We, as women, work so hard to do all the things in life well, which is wonderful, but oftentimes we push through in our own strength instead of depending on the Spirit at work in us. How do we know we are striving in our own strength instead of growing and living in grace? We begin to feel it. We become stressed and anxious, or we feel like we're never going to reach our goal. We lose a bit of our spark and joy, stuck in a try-hard mentality. Now don't get me wrong—trying hard is not a bad thing. But there must be a way to work hard and try hard, to hustle, in grace. To work hard in the Spirit, trusting His growing, transforming work inside us. I think grace-based effort stems from being so loved. As we let the truth of God's love for us sink in deeply, we are compelled to move, live, and work with His Spirit leading the way. Also, the Spirit whispers to our hearts when we are stuck in striving mode. He will give us little hints that we need to let go a bit instead of strive harder. And God will help us: "Where can I go to escape your Spirit? Where can I flee from your presence? . . . Your hand will lead me; your right hand will hold on to me" (Ps. 139:7, 10). It may take us a while to realize it's Him trying to get our attention, but when we finally do realize, our souls will find relief as we rest in Him.

We all have good intentions about wanting to grow into the women God created us to be. We all have specific ways we want to love better and to live out the callings God has placed on our lives. These are all beautiful desires. But today may we remember that we don't have to make all of that happen in our own power. It's not up to us to do the growing. And this should hopefully come as a great relief to us. We can let go of trying to grow ourselves and instead lean into God and trust His Spirit to work in us. We can trust Him to help us through each day, week, and year, through the counsel of His Spirit and the wisdom in His Word. We can trust Him to grow the fruit of the Spirit in us. We can trust Him to live through us. And when we let Him live through us, our lives will feel more like dancing and less like striving. More like freedom and less like restriction. More like grace and less like the tension of trying to do things perfectly. I pray you see the beauty of growing in grace today, and in turn, may your living feel a bit more like dancing.

GARDEN MOMENTS
for Your Soul

In what ways does your heart feel stuck in striving mode rather than growing in grace?

....

....

....

....

....

How can you lean back into God and experience the joy of a grace-filled life? What would that look like for you in a practical sense?

....

....

....

....

. . . . **Pray** . . . .

God, thank You for the gift of Your grace both for my salvation and my everyday life. Thank You that I don't have to grow into the woman I long to be by myself. Thank You for doing the work in me as I root my faith in Your love. Thank You for loving me so deeply and tending my heart so personally. Today help me step out of striving mode and lean back into Your grace. Show me what that looks like in a practical sense. Help me live by the Spirit instead of pushing through in my own power. Whisper to my heart when I'm in that striving

*mode and draw me back to Your grace-filled ways.
Thank You for the gift of Your Spirit and the freedom
to grow in grace. May today be a fresh beginning.*

DAY 26

Blossom

As you draw close to God, you find out who you are and who God made you to be. When you lose yourself in God, you become more fully yourself and begin to blossom into your true identity. Today allow God space to whisper into your soul how much He loves you. Allow Him space to shape your identity in Him.

And in Christ you have been brought to fullness.

COLOSSIANS 2:10 NIV

HOW WE DEFINE OUR IDENTITY affects the way we think and live. It's particularly difficult to place our identity in Christ alone when there are so many things pulling at us. Pressures to look, feel, and be good enough, to be successful, accomplished, and seen. Desires to impress, be liked, and fit in. But we keep pressing on, trying to shake off the sense that deep inside something doesn't feel quite right. I pray today brings freedom to your soul as you let the One who made you speak into your heart about your identity.

Without meaning to, we often base our identity in what we do, what we look like, or how we measure up, instead of in Christ alone. And if we're not careful, our identity shifts with the waves of trends and culture instead of staying steady in God alone. God created us with a desire to feel significant, to be seen and loved and to know who we are. It's not a bad desire; it's a God-given desire. So today I want to think of this search for identity in two ways: (1) basing our identity in Christ alone and (2) discovering the way He might want to use us. I think sometimes we can feel like taking that time is a waste or it's selfish that we have to pause and think deeply about where we are and where God has us. So we keep moving and we stay busy doing, and yet we rarely stop to just be and to check in with God. We go, go, go, exhausting ourselves instead of slowing our pace to be with our Maker. Without meaning to, our identity becomes based on how we're doing, how we're performing, and how our lives measure up. Over time, this wears down a gal's soul. She cannot keep up this pace.

This is a bit of a passion of mine—encouraging women to find out who they are by spending time with the One who made them. It's not selfish. It's beautiful. Because when you find out who you are, you blossom and dance with freedom and joy. You are no longer bound by expectations, the opinions of others, or trends. You are grounded in God's love and can live out His purposes for you in grace.

In a world driven by labels, titles, and positions, breaking free from society's mold to live securely and confidently as God's daughters can be tricky. This topic of identity is particularly difficult to navigate in a social media–driven culture, where we see so much and are so aware of what's going on around us. Now don't get me wrong, I love many things about social media. But even as a thirty-eight-year-old, grown-up gal, I find it hard to keep firmly rooted in my identity in Christ and who He's made me to be when I overcrowd my heart with everybody else's worlds. For some of us, when we crowd our hearts with images from social media, we begin to feel not quite enough. And social media can certainly stir up our sense of discontentment about who we are, how we look, and our lives in general. We must be careful not to look through the screen of our phones and the lens of social media apps for our significance and identity. Looking only to Christ can give us the solid sense of identity we long for.

I began my search for significance and identity as a young eighteen-year-old ballet dancer. Pointe shoes, tights, leotards, tutus, bobby pins, and hairspray were my go-to wardrobe most days. As all my friends were heading off to college, I was heading to Austin, Texas, to dance fulltime as a ballerina. I kept a tight schedule of ballet classes and rehearsals. I spent most nights icing my muscles and tending to the blisters on my toes. The little dorm room I lived in was quaint and homey. I loved this little space. The room had a large window that overlooked a courtyard wrapped in ivy and adorned with small iron tables and patio chairs. I knew I would be spending a lot of time out there, as my search for significance and identity began to stir in my soul. A restless feeling was creeping up, and I remember not really knowing what to do with it. It was easy to assume it was a bad feeling. But now I know—it was God stirring my heart.

My heart ached for significance, value, guidance, and purpose during this uncertain time in my life when I felt quite alone. I remember taking my journal, pen, Bible, and devotional book into the courtyard and beginning the process of realizing that those stirrings of my heart were God's way of drawing me close to Him. And this intimacy of drawing close to God, I now realize, is what gives us significance, value, and purpose. I had many options of things I could put my value in—my position in the ballet company, a number on the scale, getting the lead role—but over time I realized that none of those things would satisfy the hunger in my heart.

Sometimes I actually miss that sweet sense of intimacy I discovered with God there on that ivy-covered patio. It was just me and God—no distractions. I couldn't constantly see what was going on in others' lives, because this was before social media. It was just me and God growing close. I discovered that I could completely lean on Him to learn who I was. I would leave that time with God feeling so . . . loved. And from that place, the earthly things I had placed my significance in started to lose their appeal. Instead, I became more aware of God's heart toward me: "But you are a chosen race, a royal priesthood, a holy nation" (1 Pet. 2:9). I felt free to keep my focus on God, and from there blossom into who He created me to be.

I think that rediscovering "aloneness" with God is what this book is all about. We've talked about how it's hard to carve out alone time with Him nowadays. The struggle is real! And some of us have little ones, too, and we literally can't seem to find a quiet moment by ourselves. But as we remember the importance of this intimacy with God, we will find a way—somehow, somewhere. There is such deep satisfaction in getting completely alone with God, not only to find out who we are and to blossom into all He created us to be but also just to feel loved.

Jesus talks about solitude in Matthew 6:6: "But when you pray, go into your private room, shut your door, and pray to your Father who is in secret. And your Father who sees in secret will reward you." There's something about solitude and secrecy—just us-and-God moments—that satisfies us like nothing else. These moments meet our very human desire to be loved and seen and approved of. These moments shape us and satisfy our search for significance. So whether your alone time with God is in a closet, in a garden, or right there in the carpool line, organize your life around these sanctuary moments with Him. Because they are when you discover how much God loves you. They are when the God of the universe will whisper love notes from His Word to your heart, shape your identity, and teach you to look to Him for significance. They are when the good stuff happens. They are when true blossoming begins.

Today's verse says, "In Christ you have been brought to fullness" (Col. 2:10 NIV). Isn't fullness what we crave? We long to be fully ourselves, fully God's, fully known, fully seen, fully loved, and fully blossoming. It's *in Christ* that we find all the fullness we were made for. When you feel that restlessness that makes you question who you are and if who you are is enough, run to the secrecy of God's company. When you feel tempted to keep up with the world through an electronic screen, run to the secrecy of God's company. When you long to live in the freedom of being totally at ease with who you are, run to the secrecy of God's company. It's in this place that you will find everything you need to be who God created you to be. And it's in this place that you will find the everlasting love of God (see Jer. 31:3). It's in this place where you will begin to fully blossom as God's daughter.

GARDEN MOMENTS
for Your Soul

Describe a time when you felt the nearness of God in a tangible way.

....

....

....

....

....

How can you make space in your life for quiet you-and-God moments?

....

....

....

....

....

How can looking to God for the significance and identity you crave change you?

....

....

....

....

· · · · · · · · · **Pray** · · · · · · · · ·

Lord, thank You for being the One who shapes my identity. Thank You for the freedom to look to You for my significance. As I draw close to You, do a blossoming work in my heart that will steady my identity in You alone. Thank You for reminding me of the importance of getting alone with You. Show me how to make spending time alone with You a reality in my life. Help me look to You for security, significance, and identity.

....

....

....

....

....

....

....

....

DAY 27

Slow Your Steps

> *You don't have to be in a hurry. Slow your steps to God's pace. As you slow your steps and tune in to God, your soul will feel relief. There's no rush. Enjoy a slower pace with God and discover a deeper awareness of His presence.*

Slow down. Take a deep breath. What's the hurry?

JEREMIAH 2:25 MESSAGE

WE ARE ALWAYS IN THE PROCESS of growing, and as I have mentioned before, spiritual growth takes time. As does experiencing God in a deeper way. And in a time when we have so much at our fingertips so fast, our pace of life seems to be speeding up. We feel it when we're keeping up with our email inbox. We feel it when we're sitting in traffic trying to get to our destination on time. We feel it as we strive to meet our goals. We feel it in maintaining our busy schedules. And we feel it as we get our kiddos to school before the bell rings. We feel this sense of urgency to keep on pace. Life can feel like one big, hurried race. And the constant racing can leave our hearts feeling worn and empty.

We've all felt the wear and tear of hurry on our hearts. In the Marr household, the bottom of the stairs is a gathering place for all the things that need to be returned upstairs. I remember one particular day when I was moving quickly to conquer one thing after another. By the end of the day, a combination of shoes, hats, toothbrushes, toys, and clothes were all piled up on the bottom step. In my effort to save time and make one trip up the stairs, I attempted to balance everything in one load in my arms, along with a coffee cup in one hand and my phone in the other. About halfway up, items started tumbling out of my arms and back down the stairs, landing right where they had been. And in that moment, I thought to myself, *This is what my heart so often feels like.* I juggle so many things, rush from one activity to the next, attempt to take on more than I can actually do at once, and instead of helping me, all the juggling turns me into a tumbled mess. My heart feels worn, spread too thin, and overloaded. This combination of hurrying and juggling causes stress on the soul, weariness in the heart, and an overall sense of feeling like I'm missing out on a deeper kind of peace.

I love today's verse from Jeremiah 2:25 in *The Message*: "Slow down. Take a deep breath. What's the hurry?" What drives us to keep up our fast pace? When I really pause to think about it, I think we're driven by a desire to live life well—to get everything done, to keep things going, and to not miss out. We have an inner drive to succeed and please others by meeting their expectations. And these aren't necessarily negative desires, but when they are the driving forces of our lives, they wear us down physically, emotionally, and mentally. Hurry makes everything on our to-do list take top priority, but when we pause to think about it, those things actually push the ones that really matter down to the bottom of the list. For some reason, we naturally prioritize doing—to-do lists, going places, accomplishing—over being—loving, resting, and enjoying.

When we think about the ways of God, we can see from Scripture that He works more like a gardener than a race-car driver. Colossians 1:9–10 says, "We are asking that you may be filled with the knowledge of his will in all wisdom and spiritual understanding, so that you may walk worthy of the Lord, fully pleasing to him: bearing fruit in every good work and growing in the knowledge of God." *Walking worthy of the Lord*, *bearing fruit*, *growing*—these point our hearts to a slower pace. The gorgeous imagery and metaphors of roots, vines, fruit, and such sprinkled throughout Scripture speak of a different rhythm of life than the one we often find ourselves in. Cultivating a fruitful life takes time. Gals, we must slow our steps. There is beauty in slowing down. We find that when we give ourselves permission to grow slowly in grace, trusting God's timeline and ways for our lives, the pressure is off. And when the pressure is off, we flourish. When we slow our pace, in a way, we're surrendering. We are saying, "God, I trust You. I trust Your ways. I trust Your timeline. I trust Your work in me. I trust You with my life."

Hurrying can deplete our relationships. When we have a fast-paced mentality, we skim over the moments with our people in order to get on with the next thing. What if we slowed our steps? What if we slowed down long enough to make the person in front of us feel loved? What if we savored each minute? We're so quick to get to the next thing, and the next thing, right? But maybe we miss out on the best things when we're always in a hurry.

Second Peter 3:8–9 says, "Dear friends, don't overlook this one fact: With the Lord one day is like a thousand years, and a thousand years like one day. The Lord does not delay his promise, as some understand delay, but is patient with you." While I don't understand what time looks and feels like to God compared to how we experience it, there's something beautiful here to note. God holds time. God created time. And our times are in His hands (see Ps. 31:15 NIV). God is the keeper of time, so we can entrust our time to Him. He knows all that is on our plates. He knows the details of our day. He understands our good intentions. He's patient. Unlike myself, the gal who tends to lean more toward rushing than slowing, He's patient. And He's patient with us as we grow and become and learn. Patience isn't something we are naturally born with, although I'm sure some of us are naturally more patient than others. Galatians 5:22 reminds us that patience is one of the fruit of the Spirit that God develops in us: "But the fruit of the Spirit is love, joy, peace, *patience*."

Through Scripture we can also see that hurry is not a new problem. According to Mark 6:31, "He said to them, 'Come away by yourselves to a remote place and rest for a while.' For many people were coming and going, and they did not even have time to eat." The people were moving along so quickly that the disciples didn't have time for a good meal. I know I'm not the only gal who has been known to just grab a scoop of Goldfish crackers instead of taking time to sit down and eat a good meal. While in the moment, we feel like we're saving time, but we miss out on the good nutrition of real food. We miss out on energy and sustenance for the whole day. In our effort to save time, we miss out. In the same way, when keeping up our fast pace, we miss out on soul nourishment from God. Instead of trusting God with our time, deep down we're trying to control it all—and that's an exhausting way to live.

Let today inspire you to slow your steps—to literally slow down and let go of the rush to grow spiritually. Take some time with God to talk about the pace of your life and your expectations for spiritual growth. Ask Him to show you ways you are stuck and how you can break free. Ask Him to show you the why behind your hurried pace. Then take a deep breath and soak in the gift of a slower pace, both physically and spiritually. Sweet one, breathe in the fact that you don't have to live life at breakneck speed. This is an invitation to an even deeper, sweeter connection with God. Because when you stay with God in the present moment, entrusting the future, the details, the tasks, all of it to Him, you'll discover a new peace that can come only from Him. It's the peace of knowing He's in control. He's got you. And He's with you always.

GARDEN MOMENTS
for Your Soul

What has your pace of life felt like lately?

....

....

....

....

....

How have you been rushing the fruit of spiritual growth that you long to see in your life?

....

....

....

....

....

How can you literally slow your steps and enjoy God more deeply?

....

....

....

....

....

• • • • • • • • • **Pray** • • • • • • • • •

Lord, thank You for the reminder that I can slow down. You are the keeper of time, and my times are in Your hands. Thank You for the invitation to slow my pace in order to know You deeper, to love better, and to live less stressed. Help me literally slow my steps and entrust the details, the to-dos, and everything in between to You.

DAY 28
Simplify

God has called you to a life of simplicity. Simplicity makes room in your heart for God. Simplicity takes pressure off your heart. Simplicity keeps your soul de-stressed. Embrace the quiet life of knowing God, and reap the rewards of a simplified focus.

He brought me out to a spacious place.

PSALM 18:19

THE THEME OF SIMPLIFYING OUR LIVES runs through nearly every page of this book, but today I want to pull it out separately and encourage us to aim to live a life of simplicity. Why? Because doing so can help us operate more in tune with God. David wrote Psalm 18 as what we might call a praise song to God. He thanks God for delivering him from his enemies. David was entangled by the snares of death and operating in deep distress (vv. 4–5). He was afraid for his life and nearly suffocating from the fear and angst. "I called to the LORD in my distress, and I cried to my God for help. From his temple he heard my voice, and my cry to him reached his ears" (v. 6). God answered David's cries for help. "He reached down from on high and took hold of me; he pulled me out of deep water. . . . He brought me out to a spacious place" (vv. 16, 19). This is a beautiful picture of what God can do for us. He can pull us up out of our distress and restore our sense of peace that all is well because He is our helper.

While we aren't up against the same physical threats David was facing, we've been talking through some of the things that threaten our peace and connection with God. And these things can clearly cause us to feel distressed. They can make us feel entangled. Through David's heartfelt psalm, we see that God can and will bring us out from under the weight of the stress and into a spacious place again.

As a mom of three boys, I spend quite a bit of time watching my boys' baseball games. In fact, my fingers feel a bit numb at the moment as I try to type after spending a couple of hours out in the cold watching our oldest play. But cold or hot, I always love to cheer on our guys. Today as I watched one of our pitchers throw pitch after pitch, I was moved when, during a stressful situation (the game was tied and a couple of runners were on base), the coach caught the pitcher's eye and said, "Take a deep breath. You got this." My mama self took a deep breath with him, and on we watched as the pitcher relaxed, gathered his nerves, and successfully got the next batter out. And right then and there I thought about how similar that situation was to our walk with God.

In a similar way, God whispers to our hearts, *Take a breath. Together, we've got this.* His Word says: "Do not fear, for I am with you; do not be afraid, for I am your God. I will strengthen you; I will help you; I will hold on to you with my righteous right hand" (Isa. 41:10). And on we go in our living, gathered and sorted out. When we get back to this singular focus on Christ, we find our footing again. We are able to thrive.

In 1 Thessalonians 4:11, Paul calls us "to make it [our] ambition to lead a quiet life" (NIV). Making something our ambition means we seek to do that thing with earnestness and determination. Leading a quiet life can feel like the opposite of what our culture shouts from the rooftops. In our culture, big and more seem better, and busy feels like the goal. But like we've seen in so many instances throughout Scripture, Jesus's way is quite upside down from the world's ways. And Jesus must know that a quiet life focused on God is sweeter than any level of busyness or any amount of stuff we could gain or activity we could participate in.

In Luke 10:38–42, we see a glimpse into the lives of two women, Mary and Martha. Poor Martha. I always feel like she gets a bad rap as the busy bee. And how many of us are the same? We like to stay busy, and truly, I don't think there is anything wrong with being busy. Like I've mentioned before, busyness isn't a bad thing. And God did create us to work and live and move and create. Being busy in and of itself isn't the problem, but I think this little glimpse into Jesus's conversation with these women shows that maybe it's more of an issue of priorities: "Martha, Martha, you are worried and upset about many things, but one thing is necessary. Mary has made the right choice, and it will not be taken away from her" (vv. 41–42). When we look at the number of things each woman was focused on—*many* things for Martha and *one* thing for Mary—and how Jesus reacts to each woman, we get a peek inside Jesus's heart and His desire for us to be singularly focused on Him first and foremost. And to maybe not take on so many things. Mary chose one focus for her life: Jesus Himself. Martha, however, was focused on many different things, which led her to worry and become anxious. Jesus invites us to make Him our number one priority and our primary focus.

This takes simplifying. It takes asking ourselves the hard questions, like *What's causing me to be too busy? What's crowding my devotion to God? What's become more important than God?* These are tough questions, and our answers may all look a little bit different. Oftentimes we don't realize what things are draining us deep inside or severing our connection with God. Like we've touched on in different chapters, it could be that we are in general too busy and need to cut some things out. Maybe we need to say no to some things so that we're not living with such high stress. Or maybe a habit—scrolling through social media, surfing the internet for the next interesting read, trying to keep the house perfect, or putting our work before everything else— that is draining our joy and pushing out time with God. He will show you what's crowding your singular devotion to Him or what's distracting you from Him.

But here's what I want you to grab hold of today: a singular devotion to Christ is the sweetest and most freeing place to live. It's not missing out, it's getting in on the best— God's best for you. When we put Him first and keep Him as our main focus, we approach life with a sense of joy and freedom and focus. We love out of the love God pours into us. We operate from this sweet place of knowing God. And as we keep first things first, we nurture our connection to God, growing closer and closer to Him and being filled and empowered to live differently and more effectively.

Also know that making choices to simplify your life in order to keep your devotion to God your main thing is not always going to feel good at first. It's probably not going to feel like the popular or trendy choice. It will feel like you're going against the grain of culture. And at times it's going to feel really difficult. That's okay. See it as a choice to deepen your relationship with God. Know that while obedience—which is what this really is—is difficult, it leads to freedom. Romans 2:4 says, "God's kindness is intended to lead you to repentance." God isn't trying to restrict you. God isn't trying to make life boring. God isn't showing you things that are crowding your heart to hurt you. No, He wants more for you. He's so kind and loving that He wants the very best for you, just like a loving parent would want for their child. He doesn't want anything to disrupt the connection He has with you or for you to miss out on this intimacy with Him. He loves you that much.

So give God the little things—maybe it's social media, or overspending, or too many activities, or too much stuff—that may feel insignificant but are actually crowding your connection with Him. They may be different from what crowds my heart, and that's okay. We are each wired differently and so our hearts have different needs. Be encouraged that simplifying our lives to one thing—Christ—and giving our hearts space for Him will be life-giving because we will feel closer to God. To close today, take a look at Romans 12:1–2:

So here's what I want you to do, God helping you: Take your everyday, ordinary life—your sleeping, eating, going-to-work, and walking-around life—and place it before God as an offering. Embracing what God does for you is the best thing you can do for him. Don't become so well-adjusted to your culture that you fit into it without even thinking. Instead, fix your attention on God. You'll be changed from the inside out. Readily recognize what he wants from you, and quickly respond to it. Unlike the culture around you, always dragging you down to its level of immaturity, God brings the best out of you, develops well-formed maturity in you. (Message)

Today I pray you see the beauty of simplifying your life down to one focus: Christ. May you discover the joy of making Him your main thing.

GARDEN MOMENTS
for Your Soul

How do you want to simplify in this season in order to prioritize God?

....

....

....

....

What feels hard about simplifying? And what excites you about simplifying?

....

....

....

....

· · · · · · · · · · **Pray** · · · · · · · · ·

Lord, be my main thing. Be my number one. Thank You for showing me that making You my main thing simplifies my life. Help me see the ways I need to simplify my life to make room to cultivate my relationship with You. Help me see the beauty in simplifying and making You my primary focus.

....

....

....

....

....

....

....

....

DAY 29

Sanctuary

> *You hold God inside you. He's taken up residence right there in your heart. If you're like me, sometimes you forget. You forget that there is supernatural power living inside you. You forget that you have access to God at any moment of the day. Today see your heart as a sanctuary for Him.*

Christ lives within you.

ROMANS 8:10 NLT

REMEMBER TODAY who lives in you. Your heart holds God, which is why we have been talking so much about guarding, tending, and protecting our hearts. Let truth from Scripture keep your heart watered so that it flourishes like it was made to do. Pull the weeds of sin that creep in. Let the light of the Son in. Make room for the light of Scripture to cast rays of truth into your heart. Take pauses in your day to pray. Praying to God pours all the gunk of worry, stress, and negative thinking right out of our hearts. Be still before the Lord and let Him nurture you. This heart-tending we've been talking about throughout these pages is a lifelong process. We tend day by day, little by little. That sweet heart of yours was made to flourish. You thrive when you and God tend it together. Today think of your heart as a precious sanctuary for God.

Merriam-Webster's dictionary defines *sanctuary* as "a consecrated place, such as the ancient Hebrew temple at Jerusalem or its holy of holies" or "the most sacred part of a religious building (such as the part of a Christian church in which the altar is placed)."[1] In the Old Testament, we learn that God Himself dwelled in what was considered the most holy place in the temple. Exodus 36–40 describes the intricate detail, beauty, and order of the building of the temple. According to Exodus 40:34, "The cloud covered the tent of meeting, and the glory of the LORD filled the tabernacle." (*Tabernacle* is another word for sanctuary.) God Himself dwelled there in the tabernacle. Can you even imagine? And only the priests could enter the most holy place of the tabernacle. Hebrews 9:7–8 says, "But the high priest alone enters the second room, and he does that only once a year, and never without blood, which he offers for himself and for the sins the people had committed in ignorance. The Holy Spirit was making it clear that the way into the most holy place had not yet been disclosed while the first tabernacle was still standing." The only way to God was through a yearly ceremony by a priest.

But thankfully God didn't leave it at that. "But Christ has appeared as a high priest of the good things that have come. In the greater and more perfect tabernacle not made with hands (that is, not of this creation), he entered the most holy

219

place once for all time, not by the blood of goats and calves, but by his own blood, having obtained eternal redemption" (vv. 11–12). Jesus changed everything. God sent His Son so that we can have full access to God at all times and also spend eternity with Him. Jesus came so that our hearts could become sanctuaries, temples, tabernacles, homes for God.

God made a way for us to have constant access to Him. Our hearts are home for the living God. Christ lives in you. Every morning when your feet hit the ground, the spark of your Creator shines bright already. Before you've even uttered a prayer, before you've opened your Bible, before you've poured your first cup of coffee, before you've looked at your calendar for the day, the light of Christ shines brightly right there in your beautiful heart. I know sometimes it feels like He's not there. I know sometimes your human nature is to forget that He resides in you. I know it's hard to feel Jesus right there in your heart in all the moments of your day, but He's there. He's there!

God's doing our day with us. He's guiding us. He's constantly with us. He never leaves us. He's working through us. He's using us for kingdom purposes. He will show us what to say. He will show us where to go. He will show us what we need to do today. It takes faith to believe He's taken up residency in our hearts. Our job? Tune in. Tune in to the spark within us. Tune in to God in us. Tune in to the Spirit that lives in us. Sometimes I still can't believe He lives in us. I totally forget! Some days I'm just happily going about my day, doing my thing, and at some point I remember—God is with me. Christ is in me. And it seems too good to be true.

Maybe today you need a too-good-to-be-true reminder. Maybe you've forgotten you have *constant* access to His light inside you. A spark is deep within you, guiding your life and loving you. The One who made you and wants to dance through life with you while holding your hand is inside you. He made you, then chose to live within you so that you would never, ever have to do life alone. Not for one minute. Not for a second. So tomorrow, the moment you step out of bed—whether you had a rough night waking up to a newborn or your heart feels heavy from a burden you can't seem to shake—know this: the One who made you is within you. The One who made you is wide awake, ready to lead you through this beautiful, purpose-filled day that's already laid out before you. The One who made you is cheering you on with loads of grace. The One who made you and made our world knows your burdens, and He's ready to carry them for you. You have His light always. Shine on for Him and with Him. Let His light and presence inside you be your constant source of joy, energy, passion, and love. Remember, sweet one, your heart is a sanctuary for God, and when you remember His presence within you, you have access to Him and to His peace at all times.

GARDEN MOMENTS
for Your Soul

How are you encouraged when you think of your heart as a sanctuary for God?

....

....

....

....

....

....

What can you do, practically speaking, to remember daily that God resides in you?

....

....

....

....

....

....

· · · · · · · · · ·   **Pray**   · · · · · · · · ·

Lord, thank You for the gift of Your Spirit. Thank You for making a way for us to have constant access to You. Thank You for loving us so much that You made a way to dwell in our hearts. Thank You for Your grace. Help me remember You dwell in the sanctuary of my heart. Help me guard this heart of mine and make room for You to invade every inch of it.

....

....

DAY 30

Return Often

As you wrap up these pages, may you be inspired to return often to the Master Gardener of your heart. May you return often for tending, pruning, soul-nourishment, and hydration for your soul. May you return over and over again to the One who tends your soul and find the sweetest refreshment.

"Return to me," declares the LORD Almighty, "and I will return to you," says the LORD Almighty.

ZECHARIAH 1:3 NIV

CAN HARDLY BELIEVE we have come to the last pages of this journey. But today I want you to know that your journey doesn't end here. This is just the beginning! I hope these days of setting aside the busyness and distractions to slow your pace, savor Scripture, and draw closer to God have changed you. I hope they have given you fresh hope and inspiration to keep returning to God, your strong center, over and over again. I hope they have inspired you to tend your heart, grow in grace, and nurture your relationship with God.

The Israelites were a crew of people who started out on their journeys full of faith but quite often gave up later. They messed up. They stepped away from God. They put other things before Him. But God always drew them back. He always wanted them back. Jeremiah 24:7 says, "I will give them a heart to know me, that I am the LORD. They will be my people, and I will be their God because they will return to me with all their heart." God is the One who does the heart changing. He's the One who pursues us, inviting us to return to Him. And as we journey on, there will be this dance of returning. We will get caught up in busyness or distractions again and feel the weight of it in our souls. We will take note of the heaviness we feel and return to God again.

We learn to run back to God. We learn that He's our source of constant refreshment. And by His grace, He always invites us back. He always welcomes us. So as you move on from these pages, remember that while we'll still get too busy, overly distracted, and overwhelmed with all the details of life, as we make room for God, He'll help us live differently. He'll do the changing, the transforming, and the growing in us.

Think of the beauty of a gal whose heart is spacious for God. Think of the fruit God will produce in her heart and character as she tunes in to His whispers and lingers in His presence. Think of the peace and joy that will overflow from the heart of a gal who has made God her main thing. Think of the beautiful garden of her life: flourishing, vibrant, fully alive, well-watered, full of light, blossoming. Think of the beauty of a gal who lives like the birds and grows like the wildflowers. Think of the beauty of a gal growing in grace, deeply rooted in God's love.

This girl is you. As you make space for God in the sanctuary of your beautiful heart, He will whisper life-giving truth to you and *deck you with wildflowers*—He'll cover you with His grace and love. He wants you to live life from this place of knowing how loved you are, and He wants to nurture the garden of your heart so that you blossom in all the beauty and grace He has for you. God wants to be your Master Gardener so that the garden of *your* life is flourishing, vibrant, fully alive, well-watered, full of light, blossoming. He wants to take what feels impossible right now and piece it together. He wants to take what feels messy and weave it into something beautiful. He wants to take what feels hard and do the heavy lifting for you. Return over and over again to your Master Gardener. He's creating something beautiful through you as you draw close to Him.

For me, writing often feels messy at first. My heart and my thoughts and my typing fingers can't seem to all gel together. But there is faith to believe that the mess will bloom into something beautiful. There is grace to mess up, start over, try, and try again. And there is coffee, because coffee helps me savor the work and enjoy the process. And there is the Word, because without it I have no music for the pages. As you journey on from here, have faith that God can bloom whatever feels messy into something beautiful as you trust in Him. Lean into His grace . . . let yourself mess up, start over, try, and try again. No perfection required. Keep the Word close to your heart and right there in your day, because

His Word satisfies like nothing else. His Word is life-giving, soul-nurturing, and everything in between. And . . . coffee, or whatever helps you slow your pace and savor God. Grab your Bible. Grab your journal. Grab your pens. Grab your tea. Keep the things that help you tune in to God close by. Be encouraged as you leap forward in faith.

I'm honestly a little sad to leave you here, my friend. I absolutely love encouraging you in your journey. It is such an honor to direct you to the One who so faithfully tends our hearts and souls. I leave you with some final notes to inspire you to continue in your journey:

May you find the deepest refreshment in God's presence.

May you know He has you.

May you trust in His unwavering love.

May you enjoy doing the things He has placed right under your toes, work hard in His strength, and trust Him with the results.

May you linger in His Word, allowing Scripture to nurture your heart, grow your faith, and purify your thoughts.

May you know that He is with you every moment.

May you settle into a deeper faith as you make space for your Maker in the sanctuary of your heart.

Remember today to take refuge in the Lord. Anytime tension rises. Anytime stress rises. Anytime your heart feels depleted. Anytime your heart feels overwhelmed. Anytime you need refueling. Anytime you need refreshment. Anytime you need to settle some angst. Anytime you need to sort out some thoughts. Anytime.

Take refuge in the Lord. Seek Him. Sit down with Him. Tell Him what's going on in your heart and mind and soul. He loves to comfort, guide, tend, shape, help, and guard your heart. Remember today to take refuge in the One who knows all your needs and is able to tend to every single one.

May you discover the richness and sweetness of knowing God deeply as you make space for Him. May you hear His whispers. May you feel His lavish love.

> You did it: you changed wild lament
> into whirling dance;
> You ripped off my black mourning band
> and decked me with wildflowers.
> I'm about to burst with song;
> I can't keep quiet about you.
> GOD, my God,
> I can't thank you enough. (Ps. 30:11–12 Message)

GARDEN MOMENTS
for Your Soul

How has this journey changed you?

....

....

....

....

....

....

Moving forward, what are some practical ways you want to cultivate your relationship with God?

....

....

....

....

....

....

· · · · · · · · · · **Pray** · · · · · · · · ·

Lord, thank You for this journey of slowing down to tune in to You. Thank You for grabbing my attention, pulling me close, and pouring Your love and refreshment into my heart and soul. I can't thank You enough. As I move forward, help me remember the importance of keeping my heart spacious for You. Help me be intentional and thoughtful about guarding and tending my heart so I can cultivate a deeper relationship with You. Give me a fresh hunger for Your beautiful Word so that I may grow deeply rooted in Your grace and truth. Help me stay tuned to the whispers of Your Spirit in me as I navigate life with You as the Master Gardener of my heart. All praise to You, sweet Lord.

ACKNOWLEDGMENTS

Jesus—This book has been stirring in my heart for quite a while. You didn't let me let this idea go. You shaped it. You inspired it. Thank You for drawing me close to Your heart over and over again. I can't thank You enough for allowing me to put words together so that hearts can know You in a deeper way. It's such a joy. All praise goes to You.

Brian, Camp, Cooper, and Colt—One of the biggest reasons I want to steady my heart, tend my soul, tune in to God, and truly flourish is so that I can love each of you well every day. You certainly love me well back. Thank you times infinity. Brian, your encouragement and support mean more to me than I can express. Thank you for believing in me. Boys, I just love being your mom. You bless me so much every single day. Thank you all for encouraging me in the final editing stages. Your cheers cheer me on!

To the Baker Books Team—Like I say again and again, I feel like I'm in such good hands. Thank you for making the publishing process smooth, inspiring, and fun! What a joy to work with you. Thank you for providing a beautiful home for my words.

Rebekah Guzman, than you for believing in my message. To Patti Brinks and the design team, thank you for so beautifully coordinating the cover and design with the message of the book.

To Dan Balow—I don't really know how to say thank you enough. You are a mentor, a guide, and the best teammate. And you love Jesus. Thank you for dreaming with me.

To Mom and Dad—Mom, you constantly point me back to God's rhythm of grace, and I am forever grateful. Dad, your support is priceless to me, and I can't wait to return to the wildflowers in Crested Butte for more inspiration.

To Granny—Thank you for your support. I am always spurred on by your sweet words of encouragement.

To my family—Every one of you, thank you for always being so supportive and encouraging.

To my sweet friends—Thank you for cheering me on. Your hugs, notes, and prayers mean the world to me.

To my endorsers—I am so grateful for your encouragement and beautiful words. Thank you for your time and investment in this book. What a blessing.

To my readers—Every single one of you. You know that thinking of you makes my heart dance. It delights me to think of you holding this book. Thank you from the bottom of my heart. May this book bless you, encourage you, inspire you, and draw you closer to the One who so dearly loves you.

NOTES

Introduction

1. Dictionary.com, s.v. "retreat," accessed July 9, 2018, http://www.dictionary.com/browse/retreat?s=t.

Day 5 Heart-Space

1. Dictionary.com, s.v. "vigilant," accessed July 10, 2018, http://www.dictionary.com/browse/vigilantly?s=t.

Day 9 Cultivate

1. Dictionary.com, s.v. "cultivate," accessed July 11, 2018, http://www.dictionary.com/browse/cultivate?s=t.

Day 15 Grow Grateful

1. Dictionary.com, s.v. "consider," accessed July 12, 2018, http://www.dictionary.com/browse/consider?s=t.

Day 19 Porch Moments

1. Lindsay O'Connor, *If Mama Goes South, We're All Going with Her* (Grand Rapids: Revell, 2003), 145.

Day 20 Dig into Your Work

1. Mark Batterson, *Draw the Circle* (Grand Rapids: Zondervan, 2012), 27.

Day 21 Tend the In-Between Moments

1. Annie Dillard, *The Writing Life* (New York: Harper Perennial, 2013), 32.

Day 22 Making Room for the Spirit

1. Hannah Whitall Smith, *The Christian's Secret to a Happy Life* (Grand Rapids: Revell, 2012), 212.

Day 29 Sanctuary

1. *Merriam-Webster*, s.v. "sanctuary," accessed July 19, 2018, https://www.merriam-webster.com/dictionary/sanctuary.

ABOUT THE AUTHOR

Sarah Beth Marr is the author of *Dreaming with God: A Bold Call to Step Out and Follow God's Lead*. Before becoming a writer, Sarah danced as a professional ballerina for over fifteen years. She eventually started a blog of devotionals for ballet dancers, which has now become a ministry to women of all ages and seasons. Her passion is encouraging women to let God fully lead their lives and to ultimately dance through life right in step with Him. Sarah is a wife, mama, and Texas girl who loves coffee, a good porch swing, her family, and her fluffy golden retriever pup.

© Meshali Mitchell

SarahBethMarr.com

Visit Sarah online to claim free
downloadables, subscribe to her blog,
and access free dancing devotionals!

    @SarahBethMarr

LIKE THIS BOOK?

Consider sharing it with others!

- Share or mention the book on your social media platforms. Use the hashtag **#WhispersandWildflowers**.

- Write a book review on your blog or on a retailer site.

- Pick up a copy for friends, family, or anyone who you think would enjoy and be challenged by its message.

- Share this message on Twitter, Instagram, or Facebook: **"I loved #WhispersandWildflowers by @SarahBethMarr // @ReadBakerBooks"**

- Recommend this book for your church, workplace, book club, or class.

- Follow Baker Books on social media and tell us what you like.

  f Facebook.com/ReadBakerBooks

  ▼ @ReadBakerBooks